My New Normal:
Surviving Suicide Loss

Anna Cambria

Dedicated to my amazing support system. I am thankful for you every day. A special thank you goes to those who, out of the kindness of their hearts, have helped contribute to the making of my book. It is hard to believe how blessed I am to have each and every one of you with me through this journey.

"The reality is that you will grieve forever. You will not 'get over' the loss of a loved one; you will learn to live with it. You will heal and you will rebuild yourself around the loss you have suffered. You will be whole again but you will never be the same again. Nor should you be the same nor would you want to"

–Elizabeth Kübler-Ross

INTRODUCTION

It is easy to believe that everyone who commits suicide is innately selfish or suffers from depression. Many would think there were warning signs that others should have been able to see. Those assumptions, however, are far from the truth. It can be a happy, loving person who takes their own life. Those left behind can feel deceived and, most likely, have questions as to why someone with a great life would do this.

After learning of Dad's first suicide attempt, my world changed. Different emotions came over me, but anger seemed to be the strongest. There were no indications that anything was *slightly* wrong. I don't believe depression was what drove Dad to suicide. Instead, he panicked; he was broke and swamped with business-related issues. These two major problems went on for months without Mom or me knowing. Not only was it all dropped onto us after his death, but we were also grieving about tragically losing Dad.

This is a very personal book and I strive to share my extraordinary story and instill hope in those who are in a similar situation. Even after a year, it still seems unbelievable that this happened. He was the last person anyone would have expected this from considering many felt he was one of the most optimistic people in this world. Everyone who met Dad knew he was a great father, husband, and friend. He got along with anyone and never said anything negative about life. That is what I want people to remember him as, not "heartless" because of his final actions. He was an incredible man yet flawed like any other human.

The hole Dad dug himself into was too much for him to handle, even when there were many other options he could have taken. He would not have broken down his confident image in order to reach out to a family member or a professional. There were also deep-rooted issues from his childhood that arose later in life. He suffered immensely at the end, which made him feel defeated. There is no second chance to tell him, "See, it does get better." I had over two decades of wonderful memories with him. I am not going to let two weeks' worth of soured memories be the ones that remain with me the rest of my life.

My childhood was perfect and I was fortunate to have been blessed with having wonderful parents. My family went on many vacations and our road trips were filled with laughter. Holidays were spent with our large extended family and my birthday parties were always over-the-top fun. On my sixth birthday, for example, we had farm animals at our house; it was the only time a horse ever walked up and down our suburban street taking kids on rides.

I would never have traded my family for anything in the world because the three of us were so close. I was an only child spoiled with attention. No one could tell who I looked more like, I was split right down the middle. Mom and I look like twins, especially with our same colored blonde/brown hair, but I also received many characteristics from Dad (apart from his 6'2" height). I had always hoped to inherit his creativity; Dad had a brilliant mind as well as an artistic side, which showed in everything he did.

The cover of my book is of great significance. Coming up with an idea for a cover was challenging. I spent weeks designing some with various pictures, but none seemed to be "the one." Mom had the idea to use the image as the cover when she walked by it. It is a painting Dad did when he was younger; it has been displayed in our garage ever since moving in. The image has symbolism now. It portrays him as a young child, looking at Earth from Heaven. The image is calming, yet mysterious.

Writing down my feelings and memories, soon after my experiences, enables me to remember them as the years pass. This book is based solely on my experiences and grieving process. Names have been changed for privacy reasons, but the story and events are all true. It is not my intention to delve deep into the complications of Dad's business problems. I am merely touching on factors that led to his mental breakdown.

People should not be afraid to approach me because I am open to answering questions. The strength within myself has allowed me to move forward and live a happy life. With no other choice but to adjust, I have learned to live with my "new normal." There will always be unanswered questions such as, "Did he try to get better after his first attempt?" and "Did he see no way out of it?" A family friend told me Dad had such a good conscience that he couldn't live with himself knowing he had hurt the people who trusted and loved him.

It is hard to plan my future when life is uncertain, but it can only go up from here. It took a while before I could, figuratively, see the light at the end of the tunnel; healing takes time. Living it over and over again through writing has helped me come to terms with this loss more because it has given me time to reflect. I fluctuated between anger and sympathy towards his torment. These once-strong emotions became weaker and formed into acceptance. That's all a natural aspect of the journey to regaining myself: who I am now and the new definition of my family.

Although this situation was devastating, I have been able to see the best of humanity and the compassion people are capable of. People can be amazing when they need to come together during hardships. Bridges mended, feuds pushed aside, and distant friends becoming close again, all for a common cause. I would never wish what I endured upon my worst enemy but, because of this tragedy, I felt love. I have grown from experience and have overcome unimaginable obstacles.

This is my story.

June 24, 2016 –11:00 am

I had high hopes for 2016. Sixteen was my lucky number, it was even on my soccer, volleyball, and basketball jersey. The year began with getting hired for a great internship in the exact field that I envisioned for my English degree: digital marketing. It was my last semester of college and I looked forward to starting a full-time career in the summer. I had recently gone on a few graduation trips, had an amazing family, a great circle of friends, and a wonderful boyfriend. A bright future was in my line of sight because my life had been fulfilled in every way.

Life, however, is unpredictable. My everlasting nightmare began on Friday, June 24, 2016. It was the day that my happy life was destroyed and could never return to normal. One phone call, a brief four-minute conversation, changed everything.

The sunny morning made for a beautiful day. I was cheerful and ready for a fun afternoon at the beach with my boyfriend, Peter. I wanted to bring boogie boards with me but forgot to ask Dad to take them down from the garage rafters before he left for work. He would not be home for a while because he had a big meeting with a company interested in acquiring the intellectual properties of his technology. They had been so impressed by Dad's ideas and product designs that they were interested in pursuing business opportunities with him.

Dad, a self-employed industrial designer, ran his own innovation business for over a decade. He had already been spending long days at his office, including weekends, so it was not unusual he left early that morning. Since Mom was still home, she assisted me with taking the boogie boards down, not an easy task for people of our 5'4" height. We pulled them by the wrist strap and they crashed onto the floor. I put them in the trunk of my car, unaware that they would not be used for the rest of the summer.

In the early afternoon, Mom received a call from a business associate, Robert, who worked at Dad's office, urging her to come by as soon as she could. "There's something going on that you should know about," he told her but refused to go into more detail until she arrived. Mom had already been planning on going down to the office later that day to meet the new partners.

She came into the living room and told me, "I'm going to head over to the office early. Enjoy the beach with Peter!" She refrained from telling me any more details, considering she wasn't certain of the severity of what Robert was talking about. Nothing seemed out of character to me. "Thanks, see you later," I replied, then continued to work on my laptop.

That call was prompted because Robert had found Dad lying on the floor, in the lab part of his office, groggy from taking what he said was "eight" Valium. He had been prescribed Valium for persistent shoulder pain. He refused to admit that the pain was because of stress and insisted it was from sleeping in an uncomfortable position on a plane during a business trip earlier in the year. The pain would not have been that severe or long-lasting if that was the sole reason. The pain often kept him up at night and Valium was the only prescription drug that worked. There only thirty pills that were five milligrams each.

After finding him, Dad asked Robert to go home

and return to the office in an hour. He, however, remained outside. When Robert saw the men driving up for the meeting, he signaled them to pull over and the men stopped. He informed them that Dad was not feeling well and that they would have to postpone; they understood and left. This meeting was crucial to Dad; it must have left a bad impression on the men to cancel that last minute.

Shortly after, Mom arrived and saw Robert out front. She pulled into the parking lot and walked towards him hastily. He told her about the Valium and that he had recently learned the business had financial problems. Dad had been keeping the financials a secret for almost a year. That was the first time he admitted it to someone; he could not even confess it to his own wife.

After their conversation, Mom grew more worried. She then climbed up the stairs to the office while Robert waited outside. The air conditioning was on full blast and all the lights were on. Oddly, the bathroom door was open with those lights on as well. Two sheets of paper were laid out on the sparse counter. She dismissed it and moved on, searching for her husband. It was eerily quiet.

She thought Dad might have left to go for a walk since she didn't see him right away. She called out to him, but no one answered. She scanned the office again and went around the back to look where their small lab was located.

Dad was on the ground with a black plastic garbage bag over his head. She yelled and ripped off the bag, trying to get her husband up off the ground. Her heart was in her throat. She immediately knew what he tried to do. He was conscious but groggy from the Valium. Mom told him that she was going to call an ambulance, but he muttered, "No, I'm fine. You don't have to," trying to talk her out of it. "If you were going to do this, I'm going to get you help," she exclaimed. Her hands were shaking so violently that it was a struggle to hold her phone to call 911. With the trauma she had just witnessed, she could not think straight.

The paramedics arrived quickly and took Dad's vitals, while a Sheriff arrived to perform an investigation. He had to ask my parents questions that were protocol after a suicide attempt. As the ambulance took Dad away, Mom gathered her things and looked at the two sheets of paper on the counter. They were two typed and signed suicide notes; one addressed to Mom and me, the other for the men who were coming to the meeting.

She walked out to her car in a daze. Everyone from the surrounding offices crowded outside, asking Mom if everything was fine. She lied and answered "Yes," although her expression said otherwise. She got into her car and followed them to the hospital. Worst of all, she now had to explain the sudden, shocking event to me.

June 24, 2016 – 1:00 pm

Back at home, music was playing in my room until I received a call from Mom. I answered, expecting a normal conversation about the meeting. However, she declared that she was on her way to the emergency room. My mind immediately went to my only living grandparent, Dad's mother, who had been released from the hospital just six days prior for a minor heart attack, "Is it Grandma?" "No…it's Dad," she replied. My jaw dropped. That news was completely unexpected. He never had any life-threatening medical issues.

A warm feeling rushed through my body. My chest and throat tightened, making it difficult to breathe. "Is he going to be OK?" "Physically, yes… mentally, no," Mom deliberately answered. She held up well but sounded numb and distant during our conversation.

Mom spared me the details and informed me that Dad had taken a lot of Valium and overdosed, so they had to call an ambulance. I was in disbelief that he, of all people, would be careless enough to abuse prescription medication. "This isn't what the father I know would do," I thought to myself, "How could he purposely do something that would require him to be taken away in an ambulance?" Things were never going to be the same from this point on. To reassure myself that I was not about to lose my father, I kept asking Mom if he would recover. She barely gave me a response.

After the call, my mood had drastically changed. The upbeat song playing from my speakers had been interrupted by a devastating call. Suddenly, music became depressing to me when it normally brought me joy. I couldn't do anything but sit in my room and think. Dad was "my hero." I looked up to him because of his accomplishments, which were brought on through hard-work and kindness. Now, I questioned that; anger overwhelmed me. I was ready to speak my mind to him. Though I believe no one should show hatred towards their parent, it was impossible for me to control it.

Multiple questions raced through my mind, "Why did Mom say he wouldn't be OK mentally?" "Did the Valium cause some sort of minor brain damage?" "Did she mean that he would need counseling on substance abuse?" Without knowing the whole story, I could only speculate. He must have been stressed with the amount of work he had to finish and all the scheduled meetings.

Anyone who knew Dad would agree that he was always optimistic about his business. Even if something didn't go as planned, he would never say anything negative about it. In Dad's mind, everything about his work had to always be positive. Every meeting went "fantastic!" and conference calls were "great!" He claimed that the company was moving forward, upward, and onward. That was not always the truth, however. Mom had accompanied Dad to a business meeting earlier in the year. He said that it went successfully, but Mom knew that they did not get the results they had strived for, though Dad acted like they did. It was confusing how everything went perfectly all of the time. To prove it to himself, and to others, that he'd be successful with everything, he reassured himself that his way was the right way.

I helplessly waited at home, praying. I wanted to

deny it and go about my day as originally planned. It was hard to imagine how the hospital visit would be. This day had turned into a tragedy, igniting a series of events that would irrevocably change my life.

I reluctantly grabbed my phone and texted Peter, who was still at work, telling him our beach plans were canceled because something had come up. Instead of telling him the story, I said that I'd explain later. The only information Mom gave me was that Dad had been under a lot of stress from the business and had to be hospitalized. Unable to wait longer for instructions, I called Mom. She told me to meet her at the hospital to grab Dad's car keys. She needed me to pick up his car at his office.

I drove in silence on the way to meet Mom. Looking around, in the other cars, people were going about their beautiful, summer day. No one knew my feelings or what I was going through; they wouldn't care anyway. They were lucky to not be experiencing the same thing. The group of teenagers in the car next to me, with their windows down, were blasting a song and dancing. The woman in the next car, dressed in business attire, could have been on her way to work, doing her normal daily routine. I would rather have been any of them than in my present situation. Watching other people go about their day-to-day lives disconnected me from reality.

I pulled up to the drop-off/pick-up zone near the entrance of the emergency room and called Mom. I did not feel mentally prepared to see my own father in the hospital, so I was glad to stay in the car for now. My stress level was so high that my chest felt tight; I tried to take slow, deep breaths. Sitting in silence, while gripping my steering wheel, I waited for Mom.

My car was parked in the same spot where we picked up Grandma just a few days ago. It was in a covered area near the entrance. A couple of older people were being wheeled out in chairs by nurses, getting into vehicles to be taken home. This was the same scene when picking up Grandma, but the feeling was different; when we picked her up, we were happy.

The sliding doors opened and Mom walked out. My nerves escalated. I lowered my window and she handed me the bundle of keys. "Did he have to get his stomach pumped?" I asked, "Are the drugs out of his system?" She kept saying that he would be fine. No answers were comforting to me until I could see how he was doing for myself. Our conversation only lasted a minute before we parted ways. Although she was still shaken up, she acted strong. I moved forward to get the car as if this was a part of my original plan for the day.

My body did not know how to react to all of this anxiety. I called my best friend Rita, who works near my house, hoping that she had left work by now. Someone needed to help me pick up the car. Both of my calls went to voicemail. She texted me soon after saying she would call me back in a few minutes. Instead of telling her it was urgent, I replied "OK." She knew there was a problem, however, because I normally wouldn't call her multiple times in a row.

During the drive back, I formulated what to say to Rita. I hoped she'd call soon so it could be over with. This would ruin her day and be completely unexpected to her. She cared for Dad too because she was like a sister to me; we had been friends since freshman year of high school. I wanted to sound all right over the phone to make her believe it wasn't severe.

Rita finally called as I was pulling into the driveway of my house. I answered, sounding out of breath, but tried to remain calm while describing the ordeal. I informed her that he took too much prescription medication from being stressed and that he had to be taken to a hospital to make sure he was OK. Rita was in complete shock and, without hesitation, dropped everything at work to come straight over.

After walking into my house, I plopped down on the couch in my living room. Anxiously waiting for Rita to come over, I sat in complete silence, drained of energy. My phone was by my side, volume on high, in case someone called. It was hard to believe the situation I was suddenly forced into.

I usually let my dogs inside the house when I get home, but I was vaguely aware of them this time. They were looking at me through the glass door, wagging their tails with happy looks on their faces. They were excited and wanted to come inside. Dogs are innocent, always having a great day, not knowing anything is wrong. One cannot help but envy their way of life sometimes. Even with them being unconditionally loving, I didn't want them by my side.

After ten minutes, Rita walked in and greeted me with a hug. I thanked her profusely for leaving work to do this huge favor. She replied, "Well you're family. Of course I'll drop work for any emergency you have." It was comforting having someone going to Dad's office with me. We went to get the car right away, so I'd be available whenever Mom needed me. I feared the moment she would call to ask me to come to the hospital.

I hadn't driven Dad's car in years and was thankful when Rita offered to do it for me. Sitting in the driver's seat, where he normally would be, seemed too heartbreaking. On the way to Dad's office, we were trying to make sense of what had happened. Rita exclaimed, "There was no way of guessing this. It's completely unexpected." She sounded confused. "My mom told me that he would recover," I reassured her. The part I left out, however, was when Mom said, "He wouldn't be OK mentally." It stuck with me because that meant that the future was not looking promising. Maybe he would no longer be able to support us or maybe he would have to go through extensive therapy.

After exiting the freeway and going down the main

road, we navigated through the streets of office buildings to get to where Dad's suite was. I had been in the area many times before but this time, seeing the building Dad's office was in was eerie; an hour ago Dad was taken away in an ambulance at that very location. In the past, Mom and I visited Dad often. Sometimes to drop off lunch, other times we were in the area and wanted to say "Hello." My parents hosted a few office parties over the years for investors; they enjoyed the night and the bountiful spread of food that covered the tables. Because of this traumatizing event, those fun memories were now tarnished. His office would never be viewed the same way again.

We pulled into the small, outdoor parking lot and found Dad's car. As we parked next to it, people from the surrounding offices were looking over. I could sense that they wanted to ask me questions. A woman walked out of her office and headed in our direction. I was not sure if she was getting into the car next to mine or if she would knock on my window to talk to me. To play it safe and avoid her, we stayed in my car with the doors closed. As she was unlocking her car, she kept glancing over at me with a sympathetic look on her face. I avoided eye-contact until she got into her car. Thankfully, she didn't try to ask me anything.

We heard her car door close and engine turn on. Once she was out of the parking lot I told Rita, "We need to be quick before people come over." It would be hard to answer a curious person's questions when I was not even sure myself what the whole story was.

Dad's car was from the early 2000s, but still in great condition. It was the car in which I learned how to drive and passed the test for my driver license in. It went on many road trips to the desert and mountains with family, friends, and our dogs. The radio had recently been replaced and enabled with Bluetooth. Dad mostly used it to call Mom to tell her that he was on his way home from work. Every afternoon, whenever Mom's ringtone went off, I knew it was him.

I followed Rita closely on the ten-minute drive home. It was strange to see someone other than Dad driving the car. Miraculously, I drove safely while my thoughts were on Dad and not the road. In addition to being mentally exhausted, my frayed nerves made it hard to focus. My car radio was off, both hands gripping tightly on the steering wheel. I tried hard not to get upset, but I wasn't sure what to feel or think when I still didn't know the whole story. The entire day, I hadn't cried because I was worried and fearful.

When we arrived back home, we went inside and sat at the kitchen table. I was exhausted and laid my head down. Rita stayed with me. Normally, we would be joking and laughing when together, but today we were quieter with somber conversations. Rita thought that getting out of the house would be a good idea, even if we only drove around the neighborhood. To distract my mind, I agreed. The thought of going to see Dad made me so nervous that my mouth was completely dry.

We got in Rita's car and went to get a drink at Starbucks. I got my favorite, a passion tea lemonade, but it was hard to appreciate. No drink or food was appetizing to me. It was almost 3:00 and I hadn't eaten since my late breakfast. I was scared of the unknown and what was about to become of my life.

Shortly after we got our drinks, Mom called. She said that it was a good time to come over to the hospital. "I will head over as soon as we get home," I told her. My stomach felt even more knotted. Rita offered to go with me but Mom wanted me to go alone. "Thank you so much, Rita. I will keep you updated." We gave each other a long hug, then I watched her drive off; I was back to being alone. This was going to be a personal matter that I was sure would eventually be public as these things often become.

The thought of telling more people that Dad was in

the hospital was dreadful. Sharing news like that is never easy, especially when it's unexpected. He was a young, athletic man with no health issues. Every day he exercised, whether it was going to the gym, on a hike, or, his favorite one of all, going on bicycle rides. We had three bikes of his in our garage; one mountain and two road bikes. He always went on rides to de-stress whenever he came home from work at lunchtime. Instead of dealing with stress-related problems at the core, he avoided anything negative by being out in nature.

Dad definitely had his family and friends convinced that he loved his work. No one ever thought of him being in pain because of his ideal career and home life. He always said how much he enjoyed being self-employed while doing what he was passionate about. People thought of him as a stress-free and happy guy. He always had a smile on his face and was full of jokes; his "dad jokes" often embarrassed me.

His business, however, required a lot of work; he felt the pressure to please others as well as make them proud. He prioritized the goals of becoming a success and receiving praise for his work. From this experience, I have learned that life is too unfair for things to be flawless all of the time. He had convinced himself otherwise. From this point on, my life was about to be far from perfect.

June 24, 2016 – 3:00 pm

Although it was a beautiful summer day outside, it was very dark in my world. Driving over to the hospital alone, for the second time that day, was terrifying. I was angry, confused, sad, and scared to come face to face with Dad for the first time since the incident. He could look and act differently, or he might even try to play it off. I kept wondering why he would ever abuse prescription medication. He never had to take anything other than vitamins; maybe he didn't know better or, possibly, had a hidden side.

I parked in the structure and made my way towards the hospital building. Upon opening the door to the emergency room, I was greeted by a tall man in security attire standing next to a metal detector. It had been many years since I visited anyone in an emergency room, so the amount of security caught me by surprise. As they extensively searched my purse, I texted Mom to let her know I was there.

Patiently, yet anxiously, I waited for someone to come to the information desk window to check me in. A minute had passed, but no one came over to ask me what I needed. Their lack of attentiveness irked me. It may not have been that long of a wait, but minutes felt like hours. After standing there without anyone noticing me, I rudely said "Hello?" until someone heard. I was angry and did not care if I came across as unfriendly. Finally, a man looked over and came to the window. He asked me for the name of the patient I was visiting and gave me an identification sticker. He then notified me that a nurse would come get me when they were ready.

The waiting room was packed that Friday afternoon, but the noise level was mild. I was lucky to find two available seats next to each other so Mom could sit near me when she came out. I wondered what everyone was there for; people are rarely in the emergency room for a good reason.

A kid's cartoon show was playing on the TV next to me, which was the only thing that could get my mind elsewhere. Cartoons are supposed to bring lighthearted laughter and joy, but only one young boy was watching it. No one else in the room seemed to be able to focus on television.

The sick, empty feeling in the pit of my stomach grew; my nerves were shot. The benefit of sitting in the waiting room was that I didn't have to face my reality. Mom eventually walked out and found me. She sat in the chair next to me while the doctors talked to Dad privately. I kept asking Mom questions, "How's he doing?" "Did they get the Valium out of his system?" "Why did he do this?" "What was he thinking?" "What's going on?" She said that she was going to let Dad tell me the whole story. "He might get emotional when he sees you," she informed me. He would easily get emotional at sad times, and this was no exception. Bracing for any news, I didn't think anything could shock me further.

What seemed like an eternity later, a nurse opened the doors and motioned for us. We got the "OK" to go into the hospital room. My heart was racing, unsure of what to expect. We followed her down the hallway to Dad's room. A curtain was blocking the room off, not a door. When the nurse pulled back the curtains to get into the small room, my heart stopped. Sitting in the hospital bed was a man who was a stranger to me, no longer my father. He seemed smaller and weaker than anyone else in the room. It was surreal seeing him in a state of vulnerability.

I had never witnessed Dad look so broken. It made me sick. This image would be engraved in my head forever. Sheepishly smiling and only briefly making eye contact, he appeared happy to see me, "Hi Pumpkin!" Pumpkin was his nickname for me ever since I was a child. He acted like everything was fine as if we were about to have a normal conversation.

Mom and I sat down in the chairs next to the bed. Once we got to talking, his mood began to change. He looked like a strong person who had "given up" and now needed to confess, but didn't have the strength to make sense of it himself. My parents talked in a serious tone. I remained silent and let them say what they had to tell me. Mom informed me that there had been financial issues that she had no knowledge of before that day. We had no money or income to support ourselves. Dad's circumstance had put us in such a large amount of debt that he could not see a way out of it. I could not believe this was true. This could mean we'd have to move and sell everything we owned.

Dad was beating around the bush when trying to get the entire story out. He was placing blame not on himself but on the stress from all aspects of the business. "I'm not afraid of death," he said to us; he also used to say that to people throughout his life. That phrase concerned others in the past, but to him, it was because he felt his life was already fulfilled.

Dad's face was pale and he was shifting around, fidgeting with the green hospital gown; he was a defeated man. His mood changed even more drastically as he put his hand up to his face to cover tears. It was impossible for me to be sympathetic. Barely getting the words out, he said, "I can't provide for my family anymore." In the past, it would make me cry if I saw my parent that distraught, but this time was different. Someone I cared about kept a big secret from his family due to embarrassment and shame. I was confused, he was not giving me direct answers about what was going on.

Mom put her hand on my leg and said, "It was a suicide attempt." Those words cut right through me. I was taken to an alternate world, a nightmare; it was an out of body experience. Dad remained silent, looking away from us. He couldn't own up to it knowing how much pain he was causing. Immediately, rage consumed me. I glared at him and yelled, "That's the most selfish thing you could do! Why would you do this to us?" As those words left my mouth, I knew that was a bad thing to say, but I became more and more irate. I didn't care. How can someone who loves his family put them through this? It was unlike him and felt like a bizarre, immature joke.

I didn't cry, neither did Mom. The three of us seemed like different people. No one knew how to process what had happened or what the next steps were. We were all looking down, avoiding eye contact. Mom held a black garbage bag, which I assumed she had used to bring his belongings in. Unbeknownst to me, it was the bag that Dad had used to cover his head. She also had the two suicide notes in her hand. She threw the bag into the trash can next to her, never wanting to see it again.

Dad illogically tried to protect us from knowing about our financial situation and was grasping for straws to keep our heads above water. He was ashamed of no longer being able to provide an income. Both the money we lived on and the investor's money had been misappropriated. "I was brainwashed," he repeated throughout our visit, claiming to be too naïve and trusting. He began using names of individuals that I had never met. It was impossible to comprehend his accusations of others when I was fixated on my father's attempt to take his own life. In my mind, this was his fault, not theirs. Even though he looked pained, I couldn't feel sorry for him. I was fuming.

Family had always come first to him, but that changed. He saw money, instead of his own life, as more important for our well-being. I couldn't believe that he would rather die, leaving Mom and me alone to clean up the mess, than face the people he wronged. He was embarrassed and knew he ruined many financially.

Assuming we would eventually be OK once his inventions became successful, Dad resorted to lying until then. He hoped there would be a large sum of money to pay everyone back through return on their investments. His inventions did have the potential to do well on the market, but now, there was not enough money to maintain their progress. We had unknowingly been living off credit cards because Dad never let Mom see the financial statements of the business. Mom thought the credit card companies who had been calling our house phone for payments were scams. Turns out they were for the credit cards he alone possessed. The relentlessness and frequency of the calls increased because no payments were made.

The amount of debt we were in was staggering. In addition to the credit cards, tens of thousands of dollars were owed to various companies and people. Mounting debts and interest payments along with issues with the board of directors created a snowball effect, which made him unable to move his company forward. He couldn't do anything without funding. He told us that days at the office would consist of staring at a computer screen, immobilized. The long, twelve-hour days were not really for work; he was upholding appearances, suffering, and planning suicide options. Sometimes, instead of going to his office, he had been going to church to pray; it was his peaceful place.

Dad assumed he was capable of doing everything on his own. He didn't bother to consult his family or professionals because he thought people would see him as a failure. He saw death as the only way out because the pain was too much. Investors would have been let down and furious. This led to doubts on future investments for a crippled company that had once seemed so promising. The investors were not strictly business; they included friends and family. The thought of facing those he was close to was too much to bear because, at the beginning, he made them promises he worked diligently to keep. People had faith in him, hoping his innovative and life-enhancing ideas would succeed.

I was lucky to have a father who was so creative. He was always thinking of new ideas that had potential to become successful. The business side, however, should have been left for someone else to handle. Money became an important goal to him, despite Mom and I never caring about becoming wealthy. Dad's intention had always been to better the lives and health of others through his inventions. His ideas for early disease and cancer detection could have saved and improved many lives. It was his life, now, that needed saving.

When a person is on suicide watch at a hospital, they have to be constantly monitored. A young nurse remained in the room on her phone, texting the entire time, never looking up from the screen. It didn't matter that someone was in the room during such a personal conversation. She could have even been texting her friends about what was going on, feeling awkward sitting through an intense conversation that she couldn't participate in.

It was as if I was talking to someone who attempted to murder my father and sabotaged my life completely. I hated him for putting us through this. Just this morning, my parents were having their usual coffee and breakfast together, now Dad was in the hospital on suicide watch. Even though it was odd that my own father had to be babysat by a nurse, it was a relief knowing that he couldn't do anything while being monitored.

The three of us promised to tell a cover story in order to keep this a secret, per Dad's wishes. If we told anyone he attempted suicide, they would think of him as a completely different person. We were worried that, by telling others the truth, he would perceive himself as weak and attempt suicide again to escape embarrassment. His own mother and my boyfriend couldn't know what really happened.

Mom stayed with Dad for a little longer. I felt selfish leaving but that environment was too negative; it was hard to process this heavy news. He caused absolute destruction. I wanted to see Peter and get my mind off everything, forgetting this ever happened. Was I supposed to act like everything was OK?

Horrible thoughts about my future flashed through my head on the quiet drive back home. If we had to move to a different city, I would leave behind everything I cared about and worked for. I might have to sell my collectibles and treasured valuables for money. There was no way of knowing what life was about to become. It was stressful keeping this burden inside of me but I held on to the small hope that Dad would see our reactions and try to get better. I didn't want to risk him being ashamed or attempt suicide again, so I did what he asked.

It would be difficult to explain why he was taken in an ambulance and had to stay multiple days in a hospital for "stress." I needed to figure out a way to appear calm and tell Rita and Peter the cover story, reassuring them that Dad would be fine, even though nothing would ever be OK for a long time. I would have to live with an internal struggle far worse than what they'd know.

It was strange being back home, alone, not knowing what to talk about with Mom when she came through the door. Physically exhausted and slightly dizzy, I laid down on the couch. I texted Rita to tell her the lie that Dad was doing fine, but he had to stay in the hospital a few more days to be monitored. I called Peter to tell him the same cover story. I have never been a good liar until this point.

Only a select few could know Dad was in the hospital, though news like that would eventually spread. All anyone would know was that his business was hurt financially and that he was stressed from work. I would have to say that a hospital stay was great for him because he could get away from his demanding job. What if someone would suspect that it was a suicide attempt?

June 24, 2016 – 6:00 pm

Feeling the urge to leave the house, I texted Mom saying Peter was picking me up. Spending time with him was the only escape from the day's events. I had no appetite, but my stomach was growling. I grabbed a handful of almonds and forced myself to eat before meeting up with him.

Peter and I drove around aimlessly and ended up in an area that had a beautiful night-time view of the city lights. The quiet and peaceful area calmed me, but my mind constantly took me back to earlier that afternoon. I kept remembering how horrible Dad looked sitting in that hospital bed, his face deprived of color and life. He looked like he had aged ten years and lost his confidence. I worried that the hospital visit was going to be one of my last vivid memories of my father. His mind might be set to do this again.

My new reality was being vigilant of every single action Dad did. We didn't know what he was capable of anymore. The ideal future that I planned for myself was no longer possible. Work needed to be done before anyone in my family could get back on their feet. Life turned into hell.

Anna Cambria

June 25, 2016 – 6:00 am

In the twenty-four hours that followed, we not only learned that we had no money, but we were buried in credit card debt and possible legal issues with the business. Worst of all, we almost lost Dad due to his inability to handle pressure. I woke up every few hours throughout the night. Each time, my body felt like it was on fire. We were about to lose everything we had worked for. Mom did not sleep a single moment that entire night. She couldn't stop shaking. She nearly lost her husband and was going to have to be the one dealing with the urgent financial ruin and all the repercussions that were to follow.

The defeated-looking man in the hospital bed was not the one who raised me. I no longer looked up to him as inspiration. It was hard to believe he actually tried to kill himself and leave the burden of everything on us. The debt owed, plus our cost of living, were going to be a challenge to pay. Dad saw no way out, but he chose wrong. Other solutions would require many compromises, but it would be worth it. Mom was even thinking that we would have to ask for financial help from family and friends. I began applying for countless jobs in various fields, hoping to hear back from any.

June 25, 2016 – 11:00 am

They moved Dad into the psychiatric ward to stay for an unspecified amount of days. Mom went while they relocated him. She told me how surreal it was to see her own husband in a place like that. To avoid the situation completely, I spent the entire day with Peter in an attempt to feel happy. My parents understood that I didn't want to be at the psychiatric ward, but they asked me to stop by the next day. I reluctantly agreed but I didn't owe him anything after what he had done to us.

Visitation hours were much different than they were at the hospital. Only a few hours in the morning and a few in the afternoon allow family and friends to briefly stop by. Due to the severity of some of their patients, regulations and rules were strict.

I tried to piece together reasons why my optimistic and loving father was admitted to a psychiatric ward. None of it made sense. Reflecting back to the previous months, I could not think of any warning signs because he always smiled and acted positively about his career. Even the night of June 23rd, my parents went out to dinner with some relatives. Nothing seemed out of the ordinary, I dropped by to say hello before meeting up with my friends at the mall.

Everyone seemed to be having a good time, even Dad. None of us knew that all the claims he made that night about the great progress of the business were a lie. Our relatives were telling him how excited they were for his success. "You could always have a good job working for your dad's business," someone told me. I optimistically replied, "That would be a lot of fun to do again." Most of my work experience from high school through college had been marketing for his products. It was the best job.

When I got up to leave, Dad acted a little strange. We always hugged goodbye, but this time he held on a little bit longer. It was enough to seem unusual, though I didn't think anything of it at the time. Maybe he thought that it would be the final time we'd see each other.

Later that night, however, I saw Dad again. We played video games in our living room. Competitive games were our favorite because we got many laughs from them. When I was younger, he spoiled me by getting me video game consoles, knowing they brought me joy. I couldn't have been more blessed with a man more kind than Dad was to me. Where was that happy man now?

June 25, 2016 – 11:00 pm

Mom called the psychiatric ward the first night Dad was there. She became frustrated when they made it seem like her request for them to go check on her husband was a big nuisance. She grew more annoyed until the nurse finally agreed to check on him. There were a few moments of silence on the phone until Mom heard "He's doing fine and is sleeping." There wasn't much relief in Mom's eyes, but we both knew that he was being monitored. Personally, I believe they may not have even checked on him. They probably told her that he was fine to ease her mind.

Again, Mom couldn't sleep because of the stress. She had been up for two days straight with flashbacks of the ordeal. I slept intermittently; for being mentally exhausted, it was hard to believe that sleep eluded me. I woke up throughout the night, immediately overwhelmed with distress. Sleep was a respite from worry.

Anna Cambria

June 26, 2016 – 11:00 am

Mom and I went to a Mass at our church in the morning. This was the first time Dad hadn't joined us; my parents attended almost every Sunday service together. After the service concluded, Mom received a call from an unknown number. She answered since Dad was allowed to call from the phone in the ward at certain times. We walked in a quiet area so she could hear better. I wasn't sure who was on the phone but, from her facial expression, I could tell that she was content with what the caller was saying.

"That was the psychologist at the hospital," Mom told me. "He feels confident letting Dad go home, believing the attempt was only a cry for help." He assured her that only about one in ten of those who attempt go on to complete the deed. Mom seemed pleased with those odds. I was scared; Dad was safer there than at home. It was as if we were about to let a stranger come live at our house.

Dad was good at convincing others that he was OK, just as he had done to everyone these past six months. It never made sense that the business was going as well as he claimed when progress wasn't being made with products in recent years. According to him, every meeting he conducted "went great," even when there didn't seem to be follow-up afterward. He looked for the best and the positives in any situation. Being unable to admit something went poorly was what led to his breakdown; he didn't like people telling him what he was doing was wrong. Little by little, things started adding up. Everything, however, was only speculation.

Mom and I were under the impression that Dad's goal, on June 24th, was for the men who were coming over for the meeting to find him, not Mom. He never wanted to make her mad or worry her, which lead to becoming so secretive. By having the men find him drowsy from the drugs and with a plastic bag over his head, they would have seen how grave the situation was. He hoped these men would pick up the pieces and deal with the business mess. They could be his salvation. In his mind, he needed to do something drastic, possibly thinking that that was the only way the men would sign a contract with him.

The dose Dad took was not lethal, which made him claim that he didn't have the intention to die. He thought that the men who were coming over for the meeting would be compassionate and sympathetic towards him; they would see how desperate he was. His end goal was for them to acquire his company and maintain the production of products. He had been presented with a wonderful opportunity with the new company, but the board of his own company prohibited him from moving forward on any deals. In his suicide note, Dad wrote, "I have been locked up from moving the company, both technically and financially until the board of directors got issues resolved."

The issues were more than he could bear mentally, physically, and financially. With this new company's help, progress could begin again. Dad yearned for his company to be built on family and friends, not corporate coldness. Money and pride, however, became the most important things to him the last few years of his life.

It was easy to blame Dad instead of understanding that something out of his control was seriously wrong. I wish I could have taken the pain away from him, but there is no way to help someone trapped inside their mind. He was not the type of person to break down his wall. When he finally did, it was too late. He said he was a failure in life and had even failed at killing himself. I would have never expected to hear those words from him. He no longer could say any positives about life. The only hope we could grasp at was if he'd be willing to accept therapy and work with us towards a better future. We were wholeheartedly committed to supporting him.

June 26, 2016 –2:00 pm

I finally got the nerve to visit Dad while he was in the ward; Mom went every minute she could. It was difficult to accept that my own father was in a place for mental illness. I wanted to be doing normal summer activities instead. There, however, was no escaping this nightmare. I could be out having a nice day, not thinking about my reality, but I would get reminders. Seeing others having a delightful day made me feel bad for myself. Why couldn't I have that life again?

The psych ward was one of the more depressing places I had ever been to, it was eerily secluded. The building was in a remote part of the hospital, towards the back of the main buildings. I had trouble finding it amongst the overgrown trees surrounding the pathway. Outside the ward, in a gated area, was a basketball court where patients could play and get some fresh air. No one was outside; the only noise was a few birds chirping from the trees.

Getting inside the building was what I imagined entering a prison to be like. While standing outside, I had to press on a speaker to call someone to the front door. Then, they had to lead me inside to get signed in. None of the workers were friendly. "Your last name?" they asked me as I was standing in front of a table with a sign in sheet. Behind the table was a large room with many people sitting around playing board games. I was not sure if they were patients or not, but Dad wasn't over there. The large window in the background had a glare, so it made it difficult to see.

All visitors have to put their possessions in a small locker and come in empty-handed. If they brought in something for a patient, nurses would have to thoroughly search it. There were endless restrictions on what one can and cannot bring inside. I brought Dad his dark blue jeans, a grey shirt, pajamas, and books. Books couldn't contain staples in the binding, as per the ward's regulations, and pajamas couldn't have a string on them. There were very few things to do while staying there, so reading would keep Dad occupied and help him escape boredom. The nurses took the items to a different area to inspect them for anything prohibited.

After the contraband check, I was let in through large, metal security doors to get in the visiting area. A nurse had to accompany any visitor being let in and out, as well as keep an eye on everyone during the visitation. When I got past the two sets of metal doors, I saw my parents. They were sitting down on a brown, plastic furniture set that was bolted to the ground. I sat in the chair next to them.

Our every move was being monitored by two people sitting in an office behind a glass window. There was no privacy. Although it was a safe space, it was hard to accept having a family member, let alone my parent, staying in a psychiatric ward. Being admitted to a place like this could be humiliating to some, but seeing the inside of it firsthand was an eye-opening experience.

I am sure Dad thought it was demeaning to be there, but it was as if he checked into a rehab facility. He looked healthier than I had seen him in a while after no longer being burdened by the lies and secrets. The color was back in his face and life was in his brown eyes. He looked ten years younger. It was promising.

Electronic devices were not allowed at the ward;

that rule disconnected him from the outside world. All the calls, emails, and concerns expressed by business partners were a major factor in his breakdown; he wasn't able to own up his mistakes to them. Admitting fault was going to be the most difficult task, yet over time, people would forgive and move on. He needed to do it for his family.

Something was slightly off. Dad acted like his normal self, laughing and joking with us, and taking everything lightheartedly. He acted positive and insinuated that he didn't feel the need to be there since the other people there were kind of "crazy." I told him, "People are put in a place like this for a reason, especially for an attempt to take their life." Trying to fight back tears proved to be impossible once I opened my mouth. I felt confused and overwhelmed. Everything had appeared normal just a few days before, and now I was in a different universe. We had to act optimistic because Dad was already talking about a great plan for the future and how life would change for the better. I didn't know if he truly felt he was on the upswing, or if he was buying time.

During the hour I spent there, I thought about how unsettling the environment was. The people staying in the psychiatric ward seemed forgotten because Mom said she was the only outside person during visitation hours. The patients there were as human as anyone else, just in need of extra attention. I couldn't help but wonder how long some of the patients had been admitted. One girl was around my age and came over to compliment me on my lace shorts. Another woman kept walking up and down the length of the hallway at a slow pace the entire time we were there.

Everything seemed bland in the brown and white color scheme. The patients' individual rooms were sparse, the only furnishing was a bed. Bathrooms needed to be opened by the nurses with a key. Showers were secure, almost baby-proofed, so people couldn't hurt themselves while alone. One lady was showering and we could hear her singing. It comforted me that everything was safe. Dad couldn't try to pull anything harmful while staying there.

I left the ward while Mom stayed behind a little longer. A nurse let me out the same way I entered. I signed out at the front desk and was able to retrieve my purse from the locker. I couldn't fully comprehend that I visited my father in a psychiatric ward because he attempted suicide. This was my new life. A life I never expected to live.

Reality hit when I returned home. Whenever my parents weren't home, it was usually because they were out on a date or Mom was over at Dad's office helping him with work. This time, they were in the hospital. I always loved having the house to myself for some alone time. During these past few days, however, it felt lonely.

The house was quiet and empty with Dad being gone. Despite that, I was concerned for when he would be released. Returning home meant getting back to work, there was a lot for him to sort out; this retreat away from the business was only temporary. He couldn't stay in the ward forever, especially because he seemed perfectly healthy. I couldn't imagine how life was going to be once he was no longer under constant surveillance. Mom and I would have to monitor his every move and location. At home, there were no security precautions or nurses to do it for us.

June 26, 2016 – 9:00 pm

Being alone with no distractions made nighttime the worst part of the day. I continued to wake up stressed. This could be one of the last nights that I spend sleeping in my room if we had to move. I had lived in the same house my entire life; it had been Mom's parents' house before my parents purchased it. My thoughts took me to a dark future.

Thoughts of secrecy and lies burned inside of me as I was laying in bed. I had been asked the same questions every day by Rita and Peter, "How is your dad doing?" and "When is he coming home?" I didn't tell them he was in a psychiatric ward. Intentionally trying to be vague, I said he was staying in the hospital for a few more days to "de-stress." "This was one of the best things to happen to him because it's a wakeup call for him to get out of his very stressful business." This, however, was the worst thing for my family. Mom and I could never fully trust Dad. The possibility of him doing this again would always be in the back of our minds.

Anna Cambria

June 27, 2016

It was another warm summer day. Dad was allowed to come home with the permission of his doctor. I don't think he minded his stay at the ward because he was away from his laptop and phone, giving him time to reflect. He preferred quiet places over loud and busy environments; one of the many things we had in common.

Earlier on this Monday afternoon, Mom went to pick Dad up. I was at home, nervous for his return, but glad he was back. When my parents walked through the door, I hugged Dad, telling him, "It's great to have you home again. We missed you and love you." Our dogs ran up and greeted him, looking overjoyed. Our golden retriever seemed to keep looking out the window a little more frequently while he was gone, sleeping closer to the front door every night.

It felt normal again, but it was hard not to have thoughts about the past few days looming over us. Life was different, but there could be a chance that he would change back to his old self through determination. Focusing on the good was the only thing I could do. He still was a loving person that cared for his family.

We encouraged him to contact his mother. He always made an effort to talk to her every day, so while he was in the hospital and couldn't call, she grew worried. I kept reassuring her that her son was fine and would be in touch with her once he was feeling better. We had told her he wasn't able to talk because he didn't have his phone on him. Saying these lies made me feel guilty, but it was for the best. Mom didn't want him to get right back to work, so we made sure he would save his necessary business updates for the following day; his mother was the only priority.

There were a lot of changes we made while Dad was in the hospital. In order to have emergency money, I sold stocks that had been passed down to me from generations of relatives. It was hard letting that go, I was planning on using those savings to make a down payment on a future house. In addition, selling my sports collectibles, old cell phones, and video games brought in money. I listened for my phone to ring about any job opportunities.

Mom and I did everything to lower our cost of living. At the grocery store, we bought only what we absolutely needed. We canceled small expenses such as magazine subscriptions and Netflix. I wouldn't be able to have those little luxuries for a long time. It was humbling, but this sudden change in life was scary. A week ago, I was perfectly content and going about life the way an average college graduate should go. Now, I was afraid to use too many paper towels.

What bothered me the most was that Dad became untrustworthy. We baby-proofed our house, beginning with prescription medication since he tried to overdose on Valium. I flushed all of the unused, prescribed pain medication and antibiotics we no longer needed. My daily medication was hidden in a safe space, I wondered how long it would have to be hidden there.

There was only so much that we could do to keep Dad away from dangerous objects. Worried they could be used for suffocation, I popped my graduation balloons and cut them up. I was even afraid to have garbage bags or ribbon in our house because they could be used for self-harm. I had no experience dealing with a suicidal person.

This wasn't going to be a temporary thing. If he wanted to try again, he'd be able to find a way. The future looked dismal.

Dad never had a gambling, drug, or drinking problem. He had never been drunk or smoked a single cigarette in his entire life. He had always taken care of his physical health, but neglected to care for his mental health; he should have confronted that early in his life. He read self-help books and referred to those when needed. I couldn't count how many books were in his office. Those books were used as an outline and were better, in his mind, than a therapist or peer telling him what to do. It was like putting a small Band-Aid on a large, deep wound; it won't heal it.

He looked up to successful individuals such as Walt Disney and Thomas Edison. These men were great figures that he strived to be like. They left an impact, and that was Dad's goal. Their accomplishments were based on creativity and innovation. They weren't given their fame and money from an inheritance and their success didn't come without struggles. Edison, however, described his struggles in a positive light: "I have not failed. I've just found 10,000 ways that won't work." Dad followed that positive example.

Many problems of Dad's were deep-rooted. He grew up convinced that his childhood was absolutely perfect, until the moment of his parents' divorce. He had been in his early teenage years and lived with his parents; his two older sisters were already married and out of the house. He loved his parents dearly and had many great memories with them; his favorite one being their long vacation to Europe which, fifty years later, he continued to talk about as if the trip had happened yesterday.

Dad's world was changed when his father left him and his mother for reasons he never understood. His father left them in debt and without support. Because of this, Dad suffered anxiety, night sweats, and loss of security. He felt betrayed by his father. He had never seen anything wrong with his parents' marriage, so the divorce came out of nowhere. It destroyed and changed him. He became free-spirited in order to escape his feelings and internal problems, never seeking professional guidance. He thought he could move on from his suffering on his own and vowed to never do anything like that to a family of his own. This traumatic event paralleled my own; my father was about to leave my mother and me to fend for ourselves. Everything came full circle.

Dad was independent early on in life and described himself as the "lone-wolf," which continued to be true as he got older. He took a lot of chances in life, such as remote camping on his own, rock climbing, and even hitchhiking when he was only a teenager. He was always a risk-taker, even on the business side.

Around 2009, he had started a new business on his own. People who were experienced business friends of his continued to offer help, but he didn't let others intervene. He wanted things done his way and couldn't handle criticism. Despite the warnings of others, he trusted complete strangers who promised him great things from large risks. While in the hospital, Dad admitted fault for trusting the wrong people, mentioning he was brainwashed by a trusted business associate he had put all his faith in.

In the suicide note, Dad apologized to everyone and wrote that he could no longer push his business forward. He had realized it earlier in the year and could see no way out of it. For lack of a better term, he knew that he "screwed over" his family and everyone with a stake in his business.

Throughout his life, Mom hated the way Dad would say, "Death is better than divorce." Divorce traumatized him, but it seems to have a parent take their own life has a worse effect. What day was it, the exact moment, that made Dad decide to commit suicide?

June 28, 2016

This was Dad's first full day back home. He had to begin contacting the business associates who deserved explanations and updating his friends on his health. Depending on the person, he either told them that he was in the hospital for stress or that he took a break from work. Nothing about a suicide attempt was mentioned. He did not want to tell anyone the truth, and we didn't push him to.

There was a huge absence when Dad wasn't home. I missed hearing his feet shuffle across the hallway hardwood floors when he walked past my room. He usually got up around 6am to let the dogs outside. On the way to the living room, he would close my bedroom door so I could continue sleeping. This was the first morning I heard that sound again; it was comforting. What I had missed even more, though, was the father I knew and loved. He was the most amazing person, and his optimism had now vanished.

Mom could sleep better now that she had him by her side, but I was more worried than ever. It wasn't a time for celebration because the challenges were only beginning. It was troubling. I fell asleep to thoughts of, "Will he still be here when I wake up in the morning?" Whenever I woke up in the middle of the night, I wanted to go check on both of my parents, but instead, I prayed everything would be all right. It was useless to convince myself that everything was fine and to just go back to sleep. I didn't have ease of mind until Dad's feet shuffled down the hallway in the morning. Life had become unnerving.

I couldn't talk or look at him without tearing up. I wished to say, "How could you do this?" or "So you don't care that you won't be here to walk me down the aisle when I get married?" but saying those things would make me cry in front of him. Never before had I thought Dad wouldn't be there to dance with me at my wedding or be there for the birth of my children; they may never meet their grandfather.

I saved a lot of inspirational quotes on my phone about being strong and overcoming suicidal thoughts. Most had themes of "knowing your worth" or "facing obstacles." I planned on sending them to Dad, but I avoided bringing up the subject. I was too afraid to talk about suicide. It was like I was brushing the topic away instead of asking questions that I needed to ask.

I convinced myself that he was going to realize, on his own, how he almost devastated my life. After his attempt, he had told Mom that his death wouldn't be a big deal for me because I had already "been launched." He tried every way to justify his actions but there was no acceptable excuse. Taking his own death lightheartedly disregarded our situation at home. Dad truly believed we would be better off without him; this shows how different his mentality had become. I wasn't only hurt by his flippant attitude, but I was angry. Everyone goes through trying times in life, but I couldn't believe I had to go through something as extreme as this.

What was even harder was that Mom and I couldn't talk about our struggle to friends or family. We couldn't tell anyone about his attempt per his request and out of our embarrassment of the stigma of suicide. I couldn't seek comfort and instead had to lie during the most difficult time. The three of us were living a double life.

Lying about the suicide attempt was a burden to

carry. A secret as dark as this couldn't be held in forever, especially from loved ones. It would be unhealthy for me to keep these strong feelings and emotions locked internally. I couldn't cry to people simply about Dad staying in the hospital for a few days "because of stress." Everyone would eventually need to learn the reason why his hospital stay affected me so much and how fearful I was. For the time being, however, I held back tears and appeared calm for the sake and love of Dad.

I had no energy to move forward and no option but to change my life. Everything that once looked positive and obtainable was no longer feasible. Every single dollar I earned would have to go towards helping pay off credit card debts Dad created, the house payment, Dad's business debt, or any other expenses none of us were capable of paying at the moment. My own graduation and hard earned money couldn't go towards my goals. Those goals became fantasies that I wouldn't be able to save up for for years to come. How could I move out and pay my own house payment when the two people who supported me for 22 years were struggling? Moving out before they were settled would be the most selfish thing I could do.

Given the severity of our financial situation, I couldn't be picky about jobs and had to take what I could get. Not only did I hate my new home life, but I could hate the new job. A happy, long-term future seemed far away when I lived day-by-day and could only focus on tomorrow.

Father's Day, just a week ago, could have been our last one together. I had bought Dad a colorful coffee mug from my graduation trip a few weeks before and gave him a framed picture of us. The picture was taken over ten years ago, right after I performed a group dance on stage. The dance show took place at our local fairgrounds and I was wearing a sparkly, white leotard. My parents were proud of me and I had a big smile in the picture. While looking at the picture after his suicide attempt, all I could think of was how he could have possibly been OK with throwing out those memories.

In the Father's Day card, I wrote about having a "Dad and Daughter Day" soon. We often did days like that growing up. They would consist of random adventures like hikes, movies at the theater, playing tourist in our own city, or, most importantly, going to our favorite place, Disneyland. When I was a kid, those were very special days. I thought he would look forward to a "Dad and Daughter Day" because we hadn't had one in a while. When he read that part in the card, he smiled and said, "Aww, thanks sweetie," but didn't seem excited about it. Clearly, his mind was on his other plans.

I could not understand how he disregarded the hardships that his family would have to bear; the burdens he created and didn't want to deal with would be dumped on those left behind. He still loved us very much, but he believed we would be better off if he was no longer around.

June 29, 2016 – 9:00 am

Dad was home alone for the first time since the attempt. Mom and I went to yoga class to get back into our normal routine. We were concerned leaving him by himself, but we couldn't live our lives watching him 24/7. "Will you stay home? How do we know you're not going to do anything while we are gone?" I overheard Mom ask. "You just have to have faith in God," he replied. That odd remark didn't reassure me. Attempting suicide is 100% in a person's own control, so it was faith in Dad we needed. He promised us he would be fine, but we did not wholeheartedly believe him.

Yoga is a great exercise for relaxation. The instructor turns off the lights and plays calming music to help everyone unwind. This time, however, was far from relaxing. I couldn't feel calm knowing Dad was alone. I was aching to get home to make sure he was OK. I kept glancing over at the clock on the wall. Time slowly inched by. My phone was on silent but the screen was facing up so I could see if anyone calls.

Halfway through class, Grandma called. Thinking it might be important, I grabbed my phone and ran out of the room to talk. She told me, "I tried calling your house phone but no one picked up. I wasn't sure if you were out and about, so I thought I'd try your cell phone." I froze. Dad was home and should have heard the phone ring. Thoughts raced through my head, "Where was he or what was he doing?" "Maybe he was in the shower and didn't hear?"

Grandma called to inform me about her cardiologist appointment, asking if Mom or I could take her to it. I tried to not show concern in my voice, but I desperately needed to find out why Dad didn't answer. She told me the details of where the doctor's office was, but I interrupted her, saying, "Don't worry, I'm available to take you, but right now I have to get back to yoga class."

Right after the call, I texted Dad: "Grandma called the house phone and said no one answered. Did you not hear it ring?" I went back to class so Mom wouldn't worry. Every few seconds, I glanced down at my screen to see if there was a reply.

As I got back to my yoga mat, Mom questioned me, "Is everything OK?" I told her, "It was Grandma. She asked if I could take her to her doctor appointment." My phone then lit up with a text. It was a weight off my chest once I got a response from Dad. He said he didn't hear the phone ring. I didn't ask him why; I was sick of acting like a concerned parent. Unless he was in the bathroom or had his headphones in, it would have been hard for him to miss the loud ring. During the remainder of the class, reality hit me; this was how my life was going to be from now on. That scare was only the beginning. We could never be at ease when Dad was home or anywhere by himself.

July 1, 2016

Dad continued to confess what had been going on the past months, all of which Mom and I were unaware. He admitted to borrowing money from his mother. She had to keep secret that her son had no income to support his family, which most likely caused her to worry. I am sure he felt guilt for being the possible cause of stress for the heart attack.

I drove Grandma to her follow-up appointment at the cardiologist. Given her weak heart, and Dad's own request, we never told her that her son was in the hospital because of an attempt to take his own life. All she knew was that he urgently needed a break from work, and it wasn't anything to panic about. I appreciated taking Grandma because I was able to spend time with her. She had always been in great spirits, especially for an 89-year-old.

When I arrived at her house, she handed me a newspaper article that she cut out. "Can you give this to your dad for me," she said, "It's an article about cancer detection, and I thought he would want to read it." One of Dad's inventions pertained to early cancer detection, so he loved learning new information. In the past, I would have gladly shown him, but there was no way I was going to give him anything that would remind him of his business situation and inability to produce the product. I stuck the article in my purse and decided to eventually throw it away. Hearing about anything business-related left a bad taste in my mouth.

I prepared answers for Grandma's inevitable questions because Mom was the one who usually took her to these appointments. "Where's your mom today?" she asked. I had to lie, nonchalantly saying, "She is busy taking care of the business while my dad is on a break from work." I didn't mention the severity of the debts or the therapy sessions that Mom had to drive Dad to. The last thing Grandma needed was to worry. One of Dad's biggest fears was losing his mother. When reflecting on this, I grew angrier. If death affected him so much, how could he think it's OK to put his family through the same pain? It was not just hypocritical, it was insanity.

On June 17th, one week to the day of the suicide attempt, we had received the news of Grandma's heart attack. Our plane had just landed at a stop home from my graduation vacation. Dad turned on his phone and noticed that he had a voicemail from his mother. He stepped aside to listen to it. The look on his face was of shock and numbness. Grandma had called days after she was admitted to the hospital when she knew we were heading home. She didn't want to worry us, nor shorten our vacation, since it was only a minor one. Dad walked back to Mom and me and relayed the message. "She's amazing because she's completely fine after having a heart attack." His face looked like it was frozen and he barely moved his lips while talking. He never liked to sound or appear weak, but I could see it this time.

It was obvious that Dad's mind was on his mother the rest of the flight home, but he tried to focus on his prayer book instead. During that trip, he had been reading it more often than ever. In retrospect, it made sense. He was trying to grow stronger in his faith, yet his mind was already set to end his life. Suicide is known to be wrong in God's eyes, but he could no longer bear the anguish he had been suffering.

While in the emergency room, Dad admitted to Mom he had been planning this suicide for two months, even finding a bridge as an option. It infuriated me to hear how well thought out it was. For my graduation trip, Dad only met up with us in Washington D.C., the last leg of the journey, because he "couldn't afford more time off" since "work was busy." He said he considered committing suicide while we were on vacation because we would be with our family that lives on the east coast. That explained why he asked us to get fully refundable return tickets. I thought it was in case we were going to extend the days of our trip.

In the pictures taken at Washington D.C., he appeared healthy and normal. We went to museums, did tours, and walked around. There was no indication that anything was even slightly "off." I will never understand how someone could hide that big of a secret for so long, especially from family.

Keeping this big secret from Grandma about her own son was heartbreaking. She was growing annoyed because she wasn't getting definite answers. She had always known that Dad was the type of person who would "get away" to escape issues. Even as a 13-year-old, he used to take his bicycle and ride for miles up the California coast without telling anyone he was leaving. He suffered a lot of stress after his parents' sudden divorce, and Grandma understood that he coped with it through escaping the problem, temporarily.

She didn't know the severity of the situation this time though. It was unlike anything Dad had ever been through. His life had become so challenging but, surprisingly, things had begun to seem normal again as the days went on. My parents were figuring out a financial strategy for the future. Dad even told us of a business opportunity with a new company. Even though he acted positive, it would be hard for him to go back to working for someone else after being self-employed for many years. The thought of going from a big private office to a small cubicle sounded depressing to him. Mom and I showed support and hoped for new beginnings.

July 2, 2016

Dad started his group therapy sessions. The only thing we could do was have faith that they would be beneficial. I was sitting on a dining chair in the kitchen after he got home from his first appointment. I asked him how it went. He said someone in the group had lost a child to suicide. It made him choke up and unable to talk about it further. He could see how suicide negatively affected the victim's family. I hoped that realization would help Dad understand what he nearly put his own family though.

He was just a human and thought he was doing what was best for his family by using credit cards to hold us over until there was money to pay off debts. As kids, many of us think of our parents as super-humans. As we grow older, we learn that they can have flaws and emotions like everyone else does. It was incredibly difficult to see my own parent in so much pain. I began to realize that I felt sorrier for Dad than I did for myself. What would be even harder for me would be seeing people mad at him. Friends, family, and business associates knew he was a great person gifted with a creative mind for innovative ideas. I had to watch someone I love suffer right in front of me. Unable to get into his mind and make him feel better, I was helpless.

Anna Cambria

July 3, 2016

My parents took on the big task of cleaning out the office; they ended the lease since we no longer could afford the extra expense each month. Mom hadn't been there since she found Dad after the attempt, which made it difficult to go back. I didn't join them because the office was where the most devastating event of my life took place. Since the situation and hospital stay were a closely held secret, my parents didn't ask anyone else to come help.

Boxes of junk that naturally accumulated over the years, technology Dad had been working on, and the typical array of office furniture had to be removed. The office was located up a flight of stairs and the weather was around 90 degrees. With only the two of them working on it, hauling everything out of the office presented a challenge.

There were dividers in the center of the room that separated the office into a small lab, Robert's work area, and the main landing area where meetings were held. Whiteboards, computers, and TV monitors surrounded the rooms and large north-facing windows looked out into the clear blue sky. Dad's past inventions, designs, awards, and accomplishments were displayed. He was even featured in magazines; one was from the UK that included a picture of me. I was always so proud of him and his achievements. People cheered him on; I had always been his biggest fan.

The dumpsters outside were filled with everything he wouldn't need. Moving forward didn't include these reminders of the past. It was like starting a new book, but I think Dad saw it as throwing out everything he had worked for the past decades. Those concepts would never come to market. After this transition, our family could move forward towards recovery and hope.

Throughout his life, Dad kept a small, red concept car that he designed in his early 20s. It was called "The Profile." He dreamed of being rich enough one day to be able to create a real-sized, working version of it. This day, however, he surprisingly threw it out. It appeared he didn't envision his dreams being fulfilled anymore.

I had always bragged about what Dad had accomplished in life. His business projects revolved around developing advanced technology in the medical field. I couldn't have been prouder of the genius he was and the big heart he had. He always showed concern for those less fortunate and tried to help them in ways that he could.

His sensitive side was obvious whenever we would visit a dog shelter. Mom would joke that he wasn't allowed to go to shelters anymore; he would start tearing up and want to come home with a new pet every time. If there wasn't a two dog licensing limit in our city, we would probably have ended up with half-a-dozen. It seems like those who suffer the most are the ones who seek to comfort others. Perhaps that was how Dad felt when looking into the eyes of shelter dogs.

Seeing Mom and me unhappy must have been hard on him. He witnessed how much chaos he caused as we scrambled for money. He probably thought it would only get worse. The secrets would come out eventually to business associates, friends, and the rest of the family. They would be just as confused and sickened as we were, but their behavior towards him would vary greatly from ours.

July 5, 2016

I was in the parenting role, constantly watching over Dad. He was a grown, 58-year-old man and I was his 22-year-old daughter who had to take away his freedoms as if he were a rebellious teenager. This was not going to be a temporary thing, years would pass and I would still worry about the possibility of a second attempt, maybe even a third or fourth. Mom and I wanted to regain faith and treat him normally, but we couldn't.

Since he had lied and hidden secrets to protect us, the trust I had in him was lost. We tracked his phone and made sure he always had it with him. His independence was taken away, but rightfully so. Even when he went around our neighborhood walking the dogs, we tracked his location. Going for a walk was a small liberty, but it stressed Mom and me. How was I supposed to live like this forever? The constant stress and worry we endured, while putting on a happy face for Dad, was taking a toll on our mental and physical health. We rarely got a decent night's sleep.

The first day we let him drive on his own was to his new "job," which was about twenty minutes away. It was the opportunity presented by the men who were scheduled to meet with him on that fateful day. They never saw the note left for them. They thought they could still go ahead with acquiring Dad's technology.

He hadn't driven a car since the morning of his suicide attempt. His car had been parked in the same place that Rita had left it, in front of our house, a little over a week ago. His car was always visible from the window in my parents' room; it unintentionally served as a constant reminder of the freedom of driving that he wasn't allowed to have.

Before Dad left the house, I turned on his phone tracking so we would have ease of mind knowing his location all day. It was nerve-racking letting him go out on his own, especially to a comparatively far distance. Watching his car drive off and disappear out of sight was unsettling. I said prayers to myself that everything was going to be OK. It nauseated me when I thought that that could be the last time I'd see him. He knew he was being monitored though, so I couldn't imagine he would do anything.

After Dad drove off, I saw Mom using her phone to view his location. She did not let it out of her sight, making sure he was headed on the right path. It was a relief once we saw that he arrived at his new workplace. He texted us, like we told him to, once he got there safely. This was the start of gaining our trust.

As the day went on, we sporadically checked up on him to ease our minds. We were thankful he was going to be surrounded by people all day, but we couldn't keep our minds on anything else. Mom made sure he didn't turn off his tracking, but I was worried that his phone would lose power if it used location sharing the entire time. He texted her positive updates throughout his day, saying what he was doing and that it was "going great!" Same as it ever was.

Towards the end of the workday, Mom came to me with her phone, very bothered. She asked me what was going on with the map. I looked at the screen and instead of a blue pin showing where he was, it was a large grey circle. Either his phone died or he turned off the tracking. We no longer knew his current location. I grew angry that this happened but scared that Dad ran off.

We called him, but after ringing, it went to voicemail. I grabbed my laptop and tried to log into his phone's online account, hoping to start the feature of "find my phone." I kept putting in possible passwords he would use, but they all failed. After trying one too many times, it locked me out. My heart sank. The password could not be reset either because I didn't know the password to get into his online email. I was praying over and over again that he would return our calls or that the tracking would turn back on. There were no other options.

We waited helplessly, our palms were sweaty. All we could do was hope there wasn't anything wrong. It was comforting to think that an area of the building may not have a cell signal. We kept talking it out, to reassure ourselves that this was a normal glitch. Minutes felt like hours.

Suddenly, Mom's phone rang. We both let out an exhale when we saw it was Dad. She answered as fast as she could. "Heading home now. The day went great!" Dad said optimistically. Mom sternly asked, "What happened with your tracking? It turned off and we didn't know where you were." "I don't know. I was probably in an area where connection cut out." Everything he said was hard to believe, so I wasn't sure what had really occurred.

My faith in Dad crumbled after his suicide attempt. I held as much trust for him as I would a stranger passing me in the street. This wasn't who he was, but sadly who he became. I constantly fluctuated between feeling positive about how the future would unfold and falling into despair. Wherever Dad went, Mom was around. Even though I had already begun to prepare for his next suicide attempt, not knowing when it would be, I distanced myself. His death would be harder on me if I spent more time with him.

My parents went to church almost every day, hoping to restore Dad's faith in his life and future. He had always been strong in his religious beliefs ever since converting to Catholicism after marrying Mom. Throughout their marriage, they continued to go to church every Sunday, even attending Mass a few days before Dad tried to take his life. Church was not the only thing he continued to do normally up until his attempt. While Mom and I were on vacation, he scheduled and went to a doctor's appointment. I didn't know why he managed his health while he planned on dying. None of it made sense to me.

Now, whenever we were texting as we would any conversation, in the back of my mind was the constant thought that he almost tried to take himself away from our family. It was the elephant in the room no one wished to address. All I could wish for was that he realized how much he would have devastated us had he been successful. I could not imagine the tragedy of losing a parent. It didn't seem like something that could happen to me. I had a perfect life.

If Dad had been more open to confronting the issues and facing his mistakes, then perhaps I would see hope for the future. He was too concerned with becoming wealthy and successful lately, the only life he saw for himself. Mom had always stuck by his side through thick and thin for 38 years, so I didn't see why he could not admit his wrong-doing to her. The only thing she got was a signed, computer-printed suicide note that read "I'm so sorry" at the end. He was too ashamed to look others in the eye and confess the truths of the past year.

July 6, 2016

I suffered with guilt and had many regrets; one was not spending enough time with Dad throughout my teenage and young adult years. He was always caring and loving towards me, but I was worried he didn't know how much I loved him. After this experience, I began talking to him more when we were together.

"I've applied to a lot of places but none of them are exactly what I want to do," I told Dad as we were sitting around the living room. "You could always start your own consulting business. You would be great at that," he said with a smile. The idea clicked in my head: that would be a great career. "Maybe you can help me get started with that this weekend," I exclaimed, looking over to see his response. "Yeah, of course I will," he said with a nod, although he didn't make eye contact. He wouldn't attempt to leave again, would he? Making plans with him could give him another goal to live for, right? He needed to be there for his own daughter, to help her through life.

Dad was the biggest supporter of my dreams. Something recent, however, stuck out to me. Back in May, he was overly congratulatory and joyful for me to graduate. Looking back, I believe he acted that way because contributing to my college graduation was his final major accomplishment. It was a proud moment for him. Both of my parents worked hard to raise me and pay my tuition. Graduating from a respectable university validated those efforts.

There were more signs that Mom and I tried to piece together. They wouldn't have been alarming at the time but made sense now. A day before the meeting on June 24th, Dad showed Mom a list of contact names and numbers written on a notecard. The list was of business associates and information about who was on the board of directors at the company. Mom thought it was strange for him to randomly show her that "just in case she needed it." It clicked with her after his attempt: he showed her the list because they were people that would be able to help with the business once he was gone. It appalled me to think that he showed his loving wife this, knowing what his future plans were.

July 7, 2016

Every night, during the past two weeks, I searched the internet about suicide, trying to ease my mind that this was just a cry for help. I was relieved to read that in most cases of suicide attempts, it's just a one-time thing, often for attention. Dad's psychiatrist even said he was confident it would not happen again. I was still worried. Dad was in far too deep. I tried to dismiss that thought even though he was the type of person to follow through with something once he put his mind to it.

It added to the pain to watch his family suffer the consequences of his behavior. He would have to look us in the eyes every day, knowing how much destruction he had caused the two people he loved more than anything.

I grew resentful toward my father, knowing that this first attempt would not be his final one. Searching online for suicide survivor blogs and support groups made me hope I would never have to be a part of one. There was a total of two testimonials written by a young adult who had lost a father to suicide. I wanted to know how they handled the death, but they hardly fit my situation. It made me feel alone. "It doesn't matter anyway," I thought in denial, "this could never happen to me, right?"

Most people on bereavement sites stated that the death of their loved one was out of the blue. Previously, I would have thought that the majority of people who committed suicide were known to be depressed or victims of mental illness. I have learned it's quite the opposite. In most cases, the family didn't have a chance to help. There are many advertisements that talk about "looking for warning signs of depression or suicidal thoughts," but there were no such signs from Dad. At least none were visible at the time.

I read stories of people who jumped off the Golden Gate Bridge in San Francisco. In some cases, people didn't die immediately from the impact but ended up drowning in the freezing cold water. There were even a few people who jumped but ended up surviving and being rescued. Those who received a second chance at life said that as they were falling, they instantly knew they made a terrible decision. One can only speculate if the people who were successful with their attempts regretted the decision right away.

I believe Dad was not one of those "thankful" people, he was in pain and saw suicide as the only way out. His second chance was more of a burden; he had to find another way. Since Mom and I now knew, we were very vigilant. It would be difficult for him to try again while we track his location. He wanted to escape the pain as soon as possible.

Dad was too hurt, embarrassed, and ashamed to face people. They'd be angry at him for what he did business-wise and to his family. Dad was wrong, people do forgive. Intrinsically, people value life over money. He was loved by many. Of course others would initially get angry at him for his business decisions, but in time, anger would lead to forgiveness and understanding.

I believe he tried to get better through therapy. In the previous sessions, he said he participated well, but we couldn't be certain of that. I was too scared to ask him if he'd attempt suicide again. There were pictures on his phone of the whiteboards inside the room where the sessions took place. Written on the whiteboards was advice for the patients. Mom found an exercise with a prompt asking patients to answer "I am sad because...," with a line after to fill in the blanks. Dad had written "...I hurt my family and put them on edge." He crossed out the word "am" in the prompt and put "was," as if he was no longer sad. This seemed like a step in the right direction.

Despite trying, he didn't like therapy enough to continue. He didn't attend his third therapy session because he "didn't need it." He had told us that most people in the group had lost loved ones and they were the ones who needed to be there, not him. It made him seem hypocritical when he was visibly distraught over those who lost a loved one to suicide; his actions almost put us through the same immeasurable pain those people were experiencing. Maybe he didn't want to witness their pain and see the truth.

In the past, Dad always sought guidance through his self-help books, and it seemed he wanted to continue that method instead. I was uncomfortable with that because it clearly hadn't helped in the past. Another therapeutic technique of his was being outside doing yard-work.

Normally, I could hear the lawn mower going off on a weekend morning while I was still laying in bed. Our dogs usually accompanied Dad out in our front yard while he worked. Today, he did yard-work, even though it was a weekday morning. Since he used it to de-stress, I didn't think much of it. I was glad he was getting back to his positive routines. He only had to be at the new company in the afternoon. They were accommodating to him.

Later that night, we played video games in the living room after enjoying dinner together. I had been tired, but Mom suggested it was too early for bed, "You guys go play your video games and I can finish cleaning up the kitchen." I agreed and turned on the console to put one of our favorite games in. Dad and I were laughing because he wasn't good at the game, but it was his favorite one to play.

Each player had to avoid knocking over brightly colored blocks, but Dad tended to accidentally knock all of them over at once. It was a lot of fun and, for a little while, life felt completely normal again.

We played the game for a few hours until I got tired and went to my bedroom to go to sleep. He stayed out in the living room to watch TV before going to bed, and by watching TV, I mean falling asleep while one of his favorite shows was on in the background. We told each other, "Goodnight, I love you," then I walked to my bed.

July 8, 2016 – 12:30 pm

July 8th was another Friday I planned on going to the beach with Peter. The boogie boards and beach bag were still in my car from two weeks ago. I changed into my beach attire after I got home from Mass with Mom. Being her parents' anniversary, she wanted to visit the mausoleum where they are laid to rest. Every Friday morning, they offer Mass. We usually attend a few of them throughout the year.

In the center of the mausoleum, there is an altar, a beautiful sounding organ, and rows of pews. The pews are right next to crypts, but there isn't a creepy presence. It is peaceful. I had been going since I was only a few months old to place flower arrangements.

Above the altar is a dome decorated with stained glass windows. It's a quiet environment where everyone is respectful. The only noises one would hear while walking around the mausoleum are the maintenance man's keys or a woman's high heels on the marble floor.

Mom said Dad acted completely normal that morning, except he had forgotten to take his lunch with him to his new job; Mom always made him amazing lunches to bring to work. He took a shower, shaved, took his vitamins, put on his work clothes, then left through the garage. I didn't hear him leaving for work, I was still asleep in my room.

The whole morning was nothing out of the ordinary, I ate breakfast and watched the local news. I acted like life was getting back to normal, even if it was going to take a lot more time. During the past few days, I had made it a point to worry less. My stress cannot control how the future will play out.

In the early afternoon, Mom left for the grocery store while I stayed home. Our next-door neighbor, Sandy, came over when she saw Mom walking outside to her car. She told Mom she had been trying to get in contact with us while we were gone all morning, but all the neighbors only had our home phone number. We had disconnected the home phone line because it was causing stress with all the credit card companies calling.

I was sitting on my bed, messaging someone from eBay that bought my old cell phone, when I heard the front door open. Mom came back inside the house. Thinking she had already returned from the store, I told her "Wow that was fast." She explained that instead of going to the store, she had been talking with Sandy outside. It looked like she was about to give me the life-altering news I was expecting for the past two weeks.

Sandy had told her that the police had been at our house while we were gone that morning. They said a car was found on the side of the freeway that was registered to our address. The police didn't give too much information to Sandy, so she wasn't told what freeway the car was on. Mom went on to say that Sandy told her, "The officers were very tight-lipped, and this does not sound good." After hearing those words, the world around me froze. I didn't know what to do with myself. "Oh no…" I replied.

My body instantly felt hot inside, but I didn't start crying. Sadly, it wasn't a surprise to me. We hadn't tracked Dad's phone the last few days because we regained some trust in him. We reluctantly gave him some freedoms back. He was supposed to be in a meeting, so we didn't feel the need to text or call him.

The police waited for us to return for over an hour, but eventually left. They even went into our backyard, trying to open doors and windows to see if any were unlocked. Officers have to go check up on families at home if there is any cause for concern, and there seemed to be.

When we got home around noon, we noticed our dogs' water bowl had been knocked over; it was strange, they had never done that before. Maybe one of our dogs knocked it over in reaction to seeing the police officers, or maybe a police officer accidentally kicked it. Just knowing all of this commotion went on at our house while we were out was frightening.

Picturing the police cars near our house, with men in uniform walking up to our doorstep, scared me. When they had to go in our backyard, our dogs were probably barking and confused as to why there were strange men there while we weren't home. I imagined the police looking through the windows, or trying to open a door to see if any were unlocked. Things would have played out much differently if we had been home. Maybe it was for the better because we were spared that trauma.

Mom called the city police while I called our family friend, Jessica. Minutes before Mom heard the news, she received a text from her that read, "Where are you?" We imagined Sandy had called her, they kept in contact since she was a former neighbor of ours.

Jessica answered the phone, sounding flustered. She knew the police were over at our house but I wasn't aware of what else Sandy told her. To avoid worrying her more than she already was, I didn't give details. I asked her to come over so we could all talk about what had been going on. She told me she was going to drive over to our house right away.

Mom notified me that the city police weren't giving her any answers. They said they would send an officer to come over but they didn't know when. I was furious that no one could tell us what was going on, even though this was an emergency. Never experiencing the death of someone so close to me made it difficult to accept; now I was facing the possibility of it. My mind was desperate for hope, as it raced to every possibility other than death.

The police could have had the wrong license plate number. Dad could have parked his car on the side of the freeway and walked away in order to clear his mind. Maybe he "ran away" to make it seem like he disappeared. He was not the man I knew anymore, so I didn't know what he would do to escape the stress of life.

I kept praying over and over again that everything was going to be fine. In complete denial, I sent his phone a message saying, "How's your day going?" with a smiley face. I couldn't accept the thought of no longer having a father at the young age of 22. It felt unreal and impossible. "Please don't be true. Please, God."

Since he didn't respond, I called his phone five times in a row. I kept expecting him to answer my calls, then I would be able to hear his optimistic voice on the other end, acting like nothing was wrong. The only response I got was his recorded voicemail. Each phone call made me lose a little more hope, so I stopped. I was experiencing the same shock as the morning of June 24th; this time, my anxiety was worse. In my heart, I knew the severity of the situation, but I needed answers.

Dad had known we wouldn't be able to call or reach him because we were at Mass at the mausoleum. Mom recalled that during the service, she was overcome with anger when she thought about how her husband almost made her a widow. She planned to say something about that to him when she got home, she was livid. I don't remember what I was thinking at that time, my emotions and feelings were already numb.

The only thing Mom and I could do for now was

wait for Jessica to come over to our house. I changed out of my beach clothes and texted Peter, once again, to cancel our plans. He sounded worried but I refrained from giving him details. I told him to go home right after work and then I would tell him when to come over. Following Dad's wishes, I still hadn't told him about the first attempt, but I would let the whole world know now for all I cared. It was time to let the truth out.

Anna Cambria

July 8, 2016 – 1:00 pm

Ever since Dad's first attempt, it had grown increasingly difficult to remember what half-truths and white lies I had told different individuals. It appeared that soon I would be able to tell everyone the same story, there would be no more lying for the sake of Dad. Mom and I had no one to turn to besides each other. The magnitude of the secret, and all the suppressed emotions, had caused anxiety. I could sense that the turmoil of the last few weeks was about to come to a close, even though I was terrified to learn the truth of where Dad was.

When Jessica got to our house, the three of us sat down on the couch in the living room. I got us all a glass of water. It was a challenging topic to discuss and one that would surely make everyone's throats dry. Mom told her the entire background story, starting with the meeting on June 24th, and what had been going on with the business's financial problems. Seeing Mom tell someone about what had truly been going on, was a large weight off my chest. Robert, with whom we had lost contact, Mom, and I were the only ones who knew of the first attempt, so this news caught Jessica off guard.

Jessica seemed to be in denial because she had known Dad for over twenty years as the cheery man who loved life. Ever since her daughter, Callie, and I had become friends at the age of three, our families went on vacations together, Disneyland trips, and attended every party each of our families had. We saw each other nearly every day and knew each other's schedules. It was hard for all three of us to fathom that we would no longer be able to do anything the same way.

We started making calls to various city and police lines. It kept getting more and more frustrating because, even though we were making dozens of calls, no one gave us answers or got back to us. I decided to call the place where Dad had said he was going to work, but we didn't have their phone number. Searching online only turned up one number. Not knowing if it was the correct one, I still called. It was important to find out if he had gone to work but no one answered. I left a voicemail mentioning Dad's name and asked if they could call me back right away. Sounding panicked, I left my phone number and said it was very urgent. After those calls, we weren't sure of what to do. We were all so powerless.

Mom had an idea and asked me to get in contact with my cousin, Michael, who works for the California Highway Patrol (CHP). I called him, told him the situation, and asked if he could run the plates on our car. I recited the plate number while he wrote it down and said he would get back to us right away. I could count on him.

I was already bracing for tragic news, as was Mom. Jessica, who was in disbelief, kept saying "I'm sure he is fine and will be walking through the front door later today." Even if he did come home, I would be angry at him for putting us through even more mayhem. Regardless, today was the turning point, no more tiptoeing around the issue. The truth needed to be told for the sake of our sanity.

July 8, 2016 – 2:30 pm

The day had grown hot, the house quiet, as we waited for Michael to call back with the information on the plates. Our air conditioning was not working and my skin was hot to the touch. Jessica's husband, Mac, came over to join us. He gave Mom and I a hug, saying the same thing: our skin felt like it was on fire. The body reacts in a variety of ways to stress. I wasn't even crying, my body went into complete shock.

Our phones were on the coffee table, facing us with the volume on high. We impatiently waited for any of them to ring. I barely remember what I was thinking or what was said during that time. Maybe nothing was said, and we just sat in silence with solemn looks on our faces. We grew impatient, yet worried for the moment my phone would ring.

Jessica continued to call the local police station, and they kept transferring her to other lines, only for someone to repeatedly assure her that officers would get back to us soon. It was so aggravating. The situation was dire, but no one seemed understanding. It was hard to tell if they didn't want to break the news to us, or if they truly didn't know answers.

I was still expecting Dad to come home at any moment and I'd hear his voice. The thought of how Mom was only 19 when she suddenly lost her father to a heart attack crept its way into my mind. It was harder, however, for me to accept a death like this than a natural one.

Finally, my phone rang. It was Michael. I took a deep breath in and hesitantly answered, bracing for the news. To my surprise, he said, "Nothing came up on the plate numbers. Are you sure those were the correct ones?" I was confused, but at the same time it gave me a little hope. Maybe this was all just a horrible coincidence? I repeated the plates, "F as in Frank, J as in jump…" Then, we realized when I originally said "J," it sounded like "A." Being flustered during the first phone call made it hard to speak clearly.

Michael said he would try again and get back to us. My heart plummeted because I no longer had that slight hope that they had the wrong car. Once again, we had to wait for that dreaded phone call. My stomach was in knots, my body sweaty. I already knew what the news would be, but we needed confirmation first.

I told Mac, Jessica, and Mom what Michael had told me, and how we still didn't have answers. The idea occurred to Mom that maybe it was better to hear the news this way. Instead of hearing it from officers who unexpectedly arrived at our door, we were going to hear it from a family member who knew Dad personally, his nephew.

Shortly after our conversation, Michael called back. Everyone grew silent. I didn't want to answer this time, so Mom did it for me. She put the phone on speaker so everyone would be able to hear what Michael had to say. He told us, "The car had been found on the freeway, parked on the center of a bridge. Someone had jumped but I can't give more information because the person hasn't been identified yet." I had finally heard it. Even though we couldn't get all of the answers, there was no doubt in my mind.

After thanking Michael and ending the call, Mom looked at me and said, "I'm sorry." That image would be engraved in my head forever. Mac and Jessica didn't know what to say, but we were lucky to have them with us so we weren't alone. Numbness and anger seem to be a body's defense mechanism against a traumatic event such as this. Anger propelled me through that initial blow. Jessica left the room to make a call to her daughter, Callie, to ask her to come be with us. We also received a text from Michael's wife, Leah. She notified us they would be over in an hour.

Callie was the first to arrive. I don't remember what anyone said, I only have images in my head of the scene. Everyone was quiet and avoiding eye contact. No one appeared to be crying, everyone was in shock and felt numb. I even considered hiding in my room to sleep. We knew we wouldn't receive word of the identification of the body until tomorrow, but we couldn't deny it was him.

July 8, 2016 – 4:00 pm

I began to feel relieved and a sense of peace. Dad was no longer suffering. I didn't have to be secretive anymore. During the past two weeks, I was constantly terrified that Dad would attempt suicide again. He could have done something while Mom and I were gone, and we would find him when we returned home. Ever since the hospital visit on the day of the attempt, I worried every single minute of every single day. Now, I would not have to live in constant fear any longer.

In my mind, we lost Dad the morning of June 24th, not on July 8th. The man on June 24th was a stranger. I couldn't imagine someone keeping that many secrets from their family who was willing to help them. It was hard to witness how defeated and ashamed he looked. He, however, had been unwilling to accept help; it was out of anyone's control. I wish I had been able to take some of that pain away, for him to be happy again, and for things to go back to normal.

Notifying others was going to be one of the hardest things I would ever have to do. Not only would it hurt me every time, but it would hurt whomever I call as well. I decided the best way to approach it would be telling the real reason behind Dad's hospital visit. Most already knew the financial situation behind it, but not the severity. I would say that he went to the hospital because he tried to commit suicide and today, he had tried again and succeeded.

I walked into my room for privacy and made a call to Peter. The first thing I said when he answered the phone was "OK, I'm going to try not to cry when I tell you this. Stay home for now and I'll call you when to come over." Barely getting the words out, I held up most of the conversation. He sounded panicked. I realized how horrible it was going to be to go through this over and over again with friends and family.

Next, I called Rita. She would take the news especially hard. Almost every day after finding out Dad was hospitalized "for stress," she would ask how he was doing. I called her, but she didn't pick up. I was glad because I didn't have to have a repeat of the dreaded conversation quite yet. I would prefer to tell people the news in increments. When Rita would see my missed call, she would assume it would be a normal conversation. She, nor anyone else, could have guessed what I was going to tell them. I didn't want to text her saying it was an emergency, so I placed my phone in my pocket, on high volume, in case she called me back.

It would be taxing to repeat the story; I was already emotionally exhausted. I walked back out to the living room where Mom informed me there was something major we were going to have to do soon. "We are going to have to go over to your grandma's house to tell her the news."

July 8, 2016 – 6:00 pm

There is never an easy approach to giving a mother news that her child has passed away, especially when it was intentional. Since Grandma was still fragile from her recent heart attack, we were afraid of causing her more heart problems. Mom decided we would show up without calling. We didn't want to cause her anxiety as she waited by herself after a phone call.

Before heading over, we notified Dad's nephew, Keith, and his wife, Sofia, and asked them if they would meet us at Grandma's house. Mom figured it would be easier for her to be surrounded by more people she loved. Keith and Sofia could be around her longer while Mom and I had to head home. She would not feel lonely that way.

It was nearing sunset, but we still had so much to do. Michael, Leah, and Mac stayed at our house while Jessica drove us; Callie accompanied us. Mom and I were not in a state of mind to drive, so we sat in the backseat together. I had done that ten-minute drive many times before, but the ride felt like it lasted a half hour this day. I wanted to get it over with. It was hard to imagine Grandma's reaction and the look on her face when she would hear that she lost her only son. She had lost a daughter nine years earlier to natural causes. Mom and I were forced to relay some of the worst news imaginable to her, right after suffering the same trauma ourselves.

My thoughts were blurred by the shock and my mind felt empty, making it hard to be coherent in the present moment. Jessica parked around the corner from Grandma's house so we could wait until Keith and Sofia arrived. We kept glancing at the end of the street, waiting for their car. The retirement neighborhood was quiet since no one was outside in the heat. The sky was getting darker as the sun got closer to the horizon. This horrible day was almost over, but it would only begin again tomorrow.

My cousins arrived within twenty minutes and parked next to us. They got out of their car and said, "I'm sorry," while giving us hugs. It was a tough moment. Mom described our story more in-depth than what she had told Keith on the phone. The six of us then walked towards Grandma's; no one spoke a word. The grim reality hit me once I saw her house. There was no turning back.

We walked up the steps and knocked on the door. When Grandma greeted us, she seemed glad to have people over to visit, but surprised by how many came. She motioned for us to come inside, leading us over to her living room. I had been over to her house countless times, but this day it had a whole different feel to it. A once comforting home seemed strange to me as if I was in an unfamiliar place.

None of us knew what to say. I certainly did not want to be the one to break the news. I relied on Mom to tell her so I wouldn't have to speak. We asked her to have a seat. She sat down in her chair, not knowing what was going on, while everyone else sat around her. I have never seen Jessica, Callie, and my cousins so quiet before. Grandma must have known it was something about Dad since he wasn't with us. I was on the couch next to her while Mom sat on the floor. She put her hand in Grandma's for comfort.

I don't recall the words Mom said, only the image of

that encounter was stored in my memory. After Mom finished talking, Grandma looked down and shook her head, repeating "oh my…" and "but he was my rock." Dad would drop everything for his mother when she needed help. He called her at least once a day to check up on her or to simply say hi. This was a role my cousin and I, her grandchildren, would now stand in for.

She looked shattered. I felt helpless. It was hard for her to process that her son would be gone. Forever. Unlike Mom and I, who had a little time to prepare, Grandma had to simultaneously learn that Dad was actually in the hospital for a suicide attempt and that he was successful on his second try. We tried to reassure her by saying how he had been suffering but was now in a better place. It was hard to justify his actions but we wanted her to know things would be OK. We would all have each other.

Mom, Jessica, Callie, and I headed back home. Keith and Sofia stayed for support. It felt horrible to leave her and go back home. The agony would only grow worse for her as the news sunk in. We told her to call her neighbor to come over, once everyone left, so she wouldn't be alone. It always broke my heart to see others distraught, especially when it was someone I cared for so much.

July 8, 2016 – 7:30 pm

I could not fathom how much my life was about to change. One by one, Mom, Leah, and Jessica started calling and telling family and friends. I only called one person, my friend Rachel, because it would be better to tell her myself. Rita had originally told her about Dad's hospital visit, but now I needed to tell her everything. I could be honest with all of my friends now.

There was silence on the other end of the line until I finished the story. "Oh Anna, I'm so sorry," Rachel kept repeating. It made me tear up, my voice began to tremble, so I wasn't able to sound strong anymore. I couldn't tell if I cried because I felt sorry for myself, or if things were starting to sink in more.

The news was going to spread quickly. I could picture the faces of others when they would find out, their mouths open from shock, unable to form words. No one could understand why or how this happened. To everyone, he had a wonderful life and could not be happier. They saw him as I had seen him before finding out about his first attempt. No one we talked to had been in a similar situation; they didn't know how to handle this news.

Mom emailed a picture to a priest from our parish, Father Alan. It was a selfie of him and Dad at our church taken three weeks prior. Dad sent Mom the picture while we were gone on vacation to show what he was up to. Father Alan and Dad both had big smiles on their faces. Dad seemed cheerful, despite the pain he was enduring.

He had texted us multiple pictures every day of the things he was doing while we were on the east coast. My favorite picture was of our dogs near the barbeque while Dad made hamburgers. The dogs were more focused on the food than posing for the camera. To our surprise, he was doing activities, such as going up to the mountains to hike, as well as being home more, despite him saying he "couldn't afford the time off" to go on vacation with us. We trusted his judgment and didn't question it. He watched our old home videos as well, probably trying to re-live good memories one last time.

In the email, Mom asked Father Alan to perform the funeral service. He replied quickly to her email, sending his condolences, and notifying us he would be out of town the following week for a Catholic retreat. He was Dad's favorite priest; he always gave great homilies and even added some humor to keep the congregation interested. To honor Dad, we decided to wait for Father Alan's return so he would be able to perform the service. The slight delay wasn't a problem, we still had so much to take care of before we could have a funeral service.

My phone suddenly rang, it was Rita. I walked into my room and took a deep breath before answering. "Hey, sorry I missed your call, what's up?" she asked. I had to get right to the point, "So my dad wasn't hospitalized for stress the other week...He was there because he attempted suicide." There was a long pause on both ends before I could gather the words to continue telling the ordeal. That was the hardest of all calls I had to handle. I repeated, "I'm sorry," feeling the need to comfort her, as she was very distraught. It was like telling her a close family member of hers passed away.

After the heartbreaking call, Callie came into my

room to tell me that she, and her parents, were leaving soon. I was still emotional and in tears after the phone call, but I dried off my eyes and walked out of my room to say goodbye. I then texted Peter to come over. Michael and Leah were leaving too but planned on being at our house the following day. There wasn't anything else we could do that night except try and sleep.

Mom went to bed while I waited for Peter to come over. I was so exhausted from the day and could barely move my arms. All the commotion was over, but reality started to sink in. This would not be over when I wake up in the morning, it would simply start all over again.

July 8, 2016 – 9:30 pm

It was late at night when, suddenly, our doorbell rang. We were not expecting anyone, especially at this hour. Peter answered for me. One of Dad's best friends, Andy, and his wife, Rochelle, were at our door with a bouquet of flowers. Andy had known Dad ever since they were coworkers over 15 years ago. After giving them hugs, I went to tell Mom we had guests. This marked the start of visitors coming over to talk about this unbelievable act.

The five of us sat around the living room. Andy felt the need to share information that no one else was aware of. Before the suicide attempt, Dad revealed a secret to him. "A few weeks ago, he had me over at his office and confided a lot to me. He told me he was completely broke…but he didn't want anyone to know about it," Andy said. Dad had not gone as far as to mention he was suicidal, or the amount of trouble he was in, but he had seemed like a different person that day.

We were unaware that Dad confessed this to any of his friends. He wasn't the type of person to break down his wall. I sat at a distance, zoning in and out of their conversation. I was imagining Dad's face during his meeting with Andy: it was the same, defeated look he had while laying in his hospital bed, he may have even had tears in his eyes. I wished I had the ability to erase that memory so I would never have to remember my own father like that.

Later, after Andy and Rochelle left, Peter took me to get In-n-Out Burger to bring back home. That was the only food I had an appetite for. I had not eaten all afternoon, even though Jessica brought over sandwiches earlier in the day. Peter and I sat down on my couch. While eating, I had the TV on in the background, muted. I could only eat small bites of my hamburger.

My mind was so mentally exhausted that it made me feel physically exhausted. I did not want to do anything except lie down and try to process my future. I never knew that it was possible to physically feel heartbreak, but it felt like a piece of my heart was missing. I thought this was all a big misunderstanding, but at the same time, Dad's permanent absence began to sink in. I cried my eyes out.

July 9, 2016 – 6:30 am

Mom's phone rang early in the morning. A man from the morgue called to tell her that the body had been identified as Dad's. Although we had already known, it was officially confirmed. They could only identify him through his fingerprints due to the condition of the body.

Dad had various possessions on him that Mom could go retrieve; an important one being his wedding ring. He also had his headphones on him. They were the headphones that he designed and successfully sold to a company almost ten years ago. Compared to other headphones, these were unique since they didn't cause hearing damage. Dad came up with the idea after I got my first iPod. He did not want me to damage my eardrums nor prevent me from being unaware of my surroundings while listening to music. Months later, he designed headphones that sit outside of your ear. The music plays clearly, they keep you aware of your surroundings, and they won't cause hearing damage. It was a brilliant, innovative design. He wore his every day.

The height of Dad's success was when his headphones were being sold worldwide. He had always hoped to die at the top of his game, but he suddenly found himself at rock bottom. He had many dreams and new ideas; it was hard to imagine that Dad would no longer be around to engineer and design new products. He wanted to die while his ideas were still alive.

July 9, 2016 – 9:00 am

Waking up in the morning brought me back to reality; sleep was the only escape. My brain still hadn't processed everything, which provoked sadness, but mostly, I felt angry that he actually committed suicide. How could he betray Mom and me after the patience and care we gave him?

Dad had solved a temporary problem with a drastic, permanent solution. Next year at this time, he will still be gone. When I get married, he will be gone. When I have children, he will be gone. He would have been there for those events if he had stayed. Instead, he abandoned Mom and me and left us with the issues he had created. We could not properly mourn; there were too many things that needed to be taken care of.

We were told what bridge Dad's car was towed from and where it was impounded. Both were located over an hour away from our house. There were two pictures of that bridge on Dad's phone, taken June 12th. He was there planning his suicide while Mom and I were on my graduation vacation, maybe even contemplating on whether to jump then or not. He even asked our pet sitter, who watches our dogs when we are on a trip, to pick them up a few days earlier than we originally agreed on. By having our pet sitter take them, he must have been close to committing suicide one of those days.

Michael and Leah offered to go pick up the car and take it to Andy's house; he would sell it for us. It was surreal letting it go, there had been many memories with it, but we could move forward without the heartache of seeing it ever again. It would take a long time to get used to the empty space in front of our house where it was usually parked. Over the next few weeks, neighbors would wonder why the car was no longer out front unless word had already got out to them. I wasn't sure how many people already knew the story, but I assumed it was more than I could imagine.

July 9, 2016 – 11:00 am

Jessica came over to our house with a mutual family friend, Sister Carol, a nun who was able to provide much needed spiritual guidance. The four of us discussed the religious aspect of Dad's death. By being the ones left behind, Mom, I, and even Jessica were left with questions such as, "Why did this happen?" and "Why would Dad do this to us?"

In our hearts, we knew that was not the person we lived with and loved. Sister Carol's insight was greatly appreciated. She called his death a "mind attack," versus something like a heart attack. He had lost his right mind, and an invisible illness killed him. There wasn't anything we could have done to prevent it; he never sought help in his hopelessness.

Towards the end of the visit, we felt a little peace. Sister Carol led us in a decade of the rosary before she left. A decade consists of one "Our Father" prayer, ten "Hail Mary" prayers, and one "Glory Be to the Father" prayer. We prayed for Dad as well as asked for strength for ourselves. We needed strength to get through the long days ahead of us. Many of the people who would be coming over would be angry and confused. They would want us to help them understand and deal with the loss better. We had to be strong for others.

Our story had spread quickly. There was no chance of keeping it a secret; our life was public. We received countless messages and calls from people wanting to express their sympathy. New messages popped up on my phone every time I checked it; some were even from acquaintances I hadn't spoken to in years. I had spent hours yesterday telling and listening to others recite the story. Family and friends helped alleviate the stress by offering to notify others for us. Some people broke down in tears right away, but most were in shock. Contacting family and friends was so tiring, and it seemed like crying became a contagious thing. When one person started crying, it made me cry.

Dad was known and loved by many. It was tough telling those who were close to my family. No one could accept that my fun-loving and positive father had committed suicide. It felt like we were talking about someone else. I did not want the way Dad died to define who he was. Like Sister Carol said, he was physically the same man but mentally a different person. It was a deadly disease that took him from my world.

Peter came over in the morning to stay with me all day. Not too long after he arrived, my two best friends, Rita and Rachel, visited for an hour. They each brought a bouquet of flowers and were dressed in all black. I was scared they, as well as others close to me, might start second-guessing who they thought Dad was. It was embarrassing to have a family member commit suicide. Telling the tragedy to their faces made the embarrassment worse.

It was humiliating how people I didn't even know had heard our story; Dad's actions would reflect on my family. I wanted everyone to think of us the same way they always had, and to know that this will not change who I am as a person. Sister Carol, Rita, and Rachel were only the beginning of the people who would be coming over to our house.

I worried there would be an article posted online or something on the local news stations. If there is a suicide in public, there could be a story about it. Thankfully, there wasn't one word about it anywhere. I was relieved others wouldn't have to find out through the media.

As the day went on, people came over with questions. Repeating the story with each new guest, re-living it all over again, only became more difficult. Our house took on an air of somberness when it used to represent a gathering place for friends and family. There had been many fun nights of pizza parties, movies, board games, or the occasional inflatable bounce house in our backyard for birthday parties. It felt like we were telling everyone a fictional story; I waited for Dad to come down the hallway, excited to socialize with the guests who were over. He was always the life of the party.

Dad got along with everyone because of his outgoing personality; his positive energy was contagious. There was always laughter in the room as he made jokes or shared funny personal stories. My favorite story he told was when my parents went on a road trip, years before I was born, and walked into a cute vintage store to look around. They asked the woman working there if there was food, but the lady was unfriendly and replied, "No." My parents began looking around, holding up items, asking how much they were. The lady would rudely reply, "It's not for sale." What they didn't realize, until after they left, was that the "store" had actually been the woman's house!

I could listen to Dad's stories multiple times and still be entertained whenever he told them. He was the best storyteller. Now, I would never hear the sound of his voice or be able to create new memories with him. We truly all had a fun life together. I even began to wonder if our dogs knew he would never return, as they have a special intuition. Without Dad, our house, although filled with people, somehow felt empty.

July 10, 2016

Every hour, our doorbell would ring. People were constantly stopping by, often unannounced. Many of them I hadn't seen in a long time or didn't recognize. We talked out the reasons why Dad would do this, in an attempt to make sense of everything. I could barely process Dad's passing myself because it was unimaginable that someone I loved could do this to me.

The hurt felt by everyone made it hard to socialize. Reality seemed to sink in once they saw Mom or me. As I opened the door to greet our guests, their faces immediately fell. The sympathetic stares were constant; I wanted to go back to being treated normally. The only one in the room that was joyful was my people-loving golden retriever. She enjoyed the stream of visitors and helped lighten the mood.

After stepping through the front door, everyone would say, "I'm sorry," while giving us long, hard hugs. People would act strong at first, but once we got talking, the tears started flowing. We made sure to have boxes of tissues on the coffee table because our guests needed them. I got in the habit of bringing each person an ice-cold water once they sat down; talking about this subject, coupled with the heat, made everyone seem dehydrated.

Our refrigerator quickly became overfilled with meat and pasta dishes from wonderful people who made us meals. The food looked wonderful and helped me regain my appetite. I had forced myself to eat the past few days; the delicious meals made it easier. Ever since Dad's first attempt, my stomach began to look underweight. The mental stress of the past few weeks had taken a physical toll.

My mind seemed to develop a defense mechanism of forgetting all the good memories with him so I didn't have to realize what an extraordinary person I was now missing from my life. Dad's friends, family, and even I bad-mouthed him. An inaccurate image of him was being created, showing him as a horrible person.

Despite this, I could not spend the rest of my life hating my father; a step to healing is forgiveness. I would have to try to understand why he did what he did; no one knew the pain he endured. Dad never worked through the problems from his childhood, which caused him problems later in life. He held everything inside and never talked about the negativities of his past.

July 11, 2016

Michael, Leah, Mom, and I went to the first mortuary appointment. We had to start the process of obtaining death certificates. We decided on cremation due to the condition of the body. Mom wished to view Dad at the morgue before the cremation began, but we all advised her not to. I had no desire to do so because I did not want my father's lifeless body as my last vision or memory of him. Additionally, since the body was not in a viewable state after falling 450 feet, Mom would have had to go through the lengthy process of getting a court order to be granted a viewing. With the steps being so involved, and after being strongly advised against it, she decided not to pursue it.

The mortuary was located a few miles away from my house. I had driven by it many times without even knowing what it was. The building held a few offices as well as a chapel for small services. It made me think of how hard it would be to sit through Dad's funeral, something I had never been prepared for. We were the only guests in the building. The quiet was unsettling and, whether by intention or not, the stillness in the offices matched the somberness.

This was my first time at a mortuary. I didn't know what to expect. A young man in a suit came down the stairs to greet us. He was cordial and shook our hands, saying, "I'm sorry for your loss." I became sick of that phrase.

He led the four of us into a room to sit down at a large table. There were water bottles around us and lots of snacks, such as candy and chips. I grabbed a water bottle because I knew I would need it. My throat would be dry during the meeting, even though I didn't plan on talking. I had no appetite for the snacks, even though they had my favorite, mini Hershey chocolate bars.

The man was professional and compassionate towards our grief. That was his job and he was good at it. It takes special kinds of people to work in a field such as this, surrounded by death and sadness every day. No one is ever glad to be there or see you because of the circumstances. "How did you get into this business?" Mom asked out of curiosity. "I grew up around this with my family, so it's normal to me," the man replied. "Sometimes I even got picked up from school in a hearse." It lightened the mood. After being around this type of work throughout his life, he continued with this as a career.

The room grew silent once the young man brought up the death certificate template on his computer. He proceeded to fill in information as we gave it to him. Right before my eyes, someone was writing a death certificate for my father. It was the closing sentence of the story of Dad's life. This was the moment that made me realize he was never coming back. I had been fortunate to not have been surrounded by deaths of loved ones, but this one was tragic and senseless.

We arranged for a second appointment to pick up the certificates and choose which urn we would want to house his "cremains." Cremains is the term for what remains of the body after cremation. In a matter of days, Dad's body would be eternally confined to an urn.

July 12, 2016

Dad's car was finally out of our lives. It only took a few days for it to sell. We had told Andy to sell it at a price he thought was reasonable in order to get rid of it quickly. I would never have to see that constant reminder parked in front of our house. Letting it go was a relief, but I wondered if I'd ever see it driving around the city. The car was the last place Dad had been alive; I couldn't imagine what he was thinking at that time. Was he at peace or considering turning back when driving to his death? The hour-long drive was plenty of time for him to think, but his mind was made up weeks ago.

The two sets of car keys also went to the man who purchased it. We thankfully no longer had to look at them; he always carried those keys in his pocket. Seeing them, much like seeing his wallet, was heart-wrenching. Every possession of his was still around the house, but he was gone.

I remember what Dad's bundle of keys sounded like; each person's has a distinct sound. Hearing them used to be a sign he was home. I could still picture the scene. The dogs would bark and barrel to the front door. Dad would open the squeaky screen door and say, in an energetic tone, "I sold all my papers!" to state that his day was productive and "fantastic" as always. Even though I was aware that he was gone, I still expected him to walk through the door any minute. From this day forward, however, his car will never be at our house again.

July 12th started off as promising, not only from the car selling, but we were fortunate to receive another blessing. After breakfast, Mom walked out to her car to run an errand, but something caught her eye. There was a white envelope on her car's windshield, kept in place by the windshield wipers. I was still eating in the kitchen when I heard Mom's footsteps coming back up the front porch steps. She opened the door and told me, "You'll never guess what I found on my car." She showed me the envelope and said, "There is one thousand dollars in here." There was no name stating who it was from, but the generosity was beyond words. With no way to personally thank them, we could only pray that God rewards them in time. It was hard to put into words how thankful I was for those who helped pay our bills.

Mom's bank accounts were frozen immediately following Dad's death, plus, we were in unimaginable debt. Out-of-town family and friends had been more than generous, sending us money for expenses simply because they wanted to help in ways they could. The graduation cards displayed were replaced by sympathy cards. "Congratulations on your big achievement! You'll be successful in life!" turned into "Sorry for your loss. You're in my thoughts and prayers." It was hard to read the sympathy cards; I could not accept that they were about my own father.

Each morning I awoke, hoping that everything had been a terrible dream, but then reality would sink in as soon as I walked into the living room. Our house smelled wonderful and looked like a florist shop. White flowers lined our shelves and tables. Multiple bouquets came through our door every day. The flower delivery man probably had the directions to our house memorized. We got to the point where we ran out of space and lost count of how many we received. Each one represented love. Thank you cards could not properly express my feelings about everyone's care. Mom kept a list so she could later write to people and thank them; it grew longer each day.

Mom and I grew closer to friends and family. There were people over before I even woke up. My mornings consisted of sleeping in until 9:30 because of my constant exhaustion. We wouldn't have spent so much time with others if this tragedy hadn't happened. I feared, however, that once the funeral was over, help and generosity from others would slowly fade. Most people would forget while Mom and I would be stuck forever with the aftermath. Focusing on the present, instead of worrying about the future, was all we could do; there was a lot of work to be done in the meantime.

Although the day started off wonderful, others can make the rest of it miserable. We learned a new problem was finding out where much of the investors' money went. Men, whose names I only recognized because I had heard Dad speak of them, were calling to figure out what was going to happen with the business. Mom would receive a call every time we were driving around in her car. The music would pause, her ringtone would start, and we immediately tensed. The legal mess was unbelievable, but it was made worse because they refused to allow us time to grieve and recover. For them, it was business as usual.

The associates were adamant about knowing right away about the debts and how anyone could rebuild the lost prototypes of Dad's products. The prototypes were in the hands of someone who wasn't returning them to the company. They were also fighting with one another because it was unclear who owned the rights to certain technologies. Had Dad wrongly given each of these rights to more than one person? It was chaos.

During the last few months of Dad's life, people

had grown furious with him. He was not able to handle it and knew things would only get worse. Investors and associates didn't know what was going on. They pressured him for updates about the progress of the company. There was nothing to show because of the roadblocks Dad had hit and didn't tell anyone about. He never had devious intentions, he just got to a point where he didn't know what to do anymore and became desperate.

The past week, I continuously heard awful updates. The emails that business investors wrote to Mom were strongly worded. Hearing cruel words being said about my own father did not bother me, I was as mad as they were. He was previously liked by so many, the tides quickly turned on him. Everyone put all the blame on Dad and didn't think about why he chose to take his life. People were mad for different reasons: he devastated Mom and me, he left the business in debt, or that he acted dishonestly. Most did not know how to express their hatred; the displaced anger went towards Mom.

Dinner conversations were consistently about Dad. It seemed like there was nothing else we were allowed to talk about. I could not avoid the topic like I did during the two weeks after the attempt. This was the reality we had to get through together. We needed to try to make sense of everything. "It's unbelievable that he would actually do this," Mom and I repeated each conversation. We were angered that he didn't want to do what was right and try to get better for the sake of his family. Why couldn't he "man up" and face everyone with the truth?

July 13, 2016

Michael, Leah, and their sons, Cody and Mark, came down to our house every day that first week, a two hour round trip drive. I wasn't sure what we would do without their constant support. They helped with yard work, cleaning around the house, and coming up with plans for the future, such as obtaining death certificates, making appointments at the mortuary and mausoleum, and a game plan for the future of our finances, just to name a few.

Michael and Leah joined us for our second appointment at the mortuary when we had to pick out the urn. As we entered the building, the same young man came out to greet us. We went back into the room, but this time, it had a different feel to it. Dad's death had begun to sink in more. This was for my father and not a fake ceremony in my nightmare. The man turned on a monitor where there was a large selection of urns. He scrolled through each one individually.

We came across many that seemed like the perfect choice, some were tall and we weren't sure if they would fit inside a niche. After narrowing it down between multiple choices, we decided on a sand-colored marble urn. We chose the color because he loved the beach. That urn, pictured on the TV screen, was what the rest of Dad's body would be confined to forever. He would no longer be a 6'2" man with a large spirit inside of him. Death is an inevitable part of life but, as a child, I thought my parents would live forever.

Mom and I didn't want to go back and re-live soured memories, so there were certain things that people helped with. The two of us wanted nothing to do with Dad's old office, but there were still items there that needed to be taken out and brought over to our house. Mac and Jessica met my cousin Keith at the office. They dealt with the remainder of throwing out or donating anything they knew was unnecessary to keep.

Mac and Jessica pulled into our driveway, their car filled with boxes and poster boards. I couldn't even go out there to help. Seeing Dad's ideas and notes would have taken an emotional toll on me. I had seen those poster boards he created to display his products multiple times, but seeing those now broke my heart. He worked hard for success but, in the end, saw himself as a failure. I stayed inside the house while Mom and Peter accompanied Mac and Jessica in unloading their car. Our garage reached maximum capacity.

Twenty cardboard moving boxes, filled with files of paperwork and photographs of old inventions, were stacked in our garage until we could move them to a safe, storage facility. After Mac and Jessica left, we did a brief search through the contents; thoroughly looking through everything would take an entire day. We hoped to find documents that could be considered important for the business's future success or the possible trials if no agreement can be reached. There was no direct trail for anyone to follow, so it was critical to find anything useful.

Helpful business partners were struggling to find a way to reverse engineer Dad's innovations with what information we had. Afraid that his intellectual properties would be copied, Dad hadn't shared crucial information with others; many were at a loss of what they could salvage.

We had recently added a reliable lock to the side door in the garage so the boxes could be protected from possible theft. We were overly cautious about important business documents because we weren't sure who to trust; Dad said that he himself was not to blame for the corruption in the business.

Mom was out of the house in the evening while I was with Peter at home. I heard our doorbell ring. My eyes were red from crying, so I sent Peter to answer the door for me. It was my neighbor, Debora. She had brought over dinner for Mom and me. She had made us so much food that she couldn't carry it all on her own. Peter walked down the street with her to get the rest of the food. I felt rude not helping. It had been hard to talk to others because, not only was I crying most of the time, but the situation was embarrassing. Suicide had a big stigma to it, and I was worried it was reflecting on my family. I hoped people would understand why I wasn't willing to socialize.

Peter and Debora came back with the remainder of the dinner. I came out to see a beautiful selection of enchiladas, rice, beans, and salad. That was the first night I had an appetite. The small gesture of her making us dinner made a difference. It freed Mom and me from that responsibility, but more importantly, it showed people were thinking of us.

I thanked Debora and gave her a hug on the way out. Neighbors, friends, and family helped take care of me every day. If only Dad was able to be here and see the good in humanity, the opposite of what he experienced during the last year, he may have changed his perspective on life.

July 14, 2016

After our relaxing yoga class in the morning, Mom received a text from the mortuary:

"Just wanted to let you know that [the] cremation ended an hour ago. I should have him back in my care either today or tomorrow. All we are waiting on now is the death certificates and the urn. I should be expecting both sometime mid next week. I will let you know as soon as everything has arrived, so we can schedule a time for your family to come and get [him].
Have a Wonderful Day!"

We found comedy in that message when it said, "Have a Wonderful Day!" The man had just relayed a message to Mom that her husband's body had been cremated and told her to have a wonderful day. We were able to laugh and joke about it for hours. As dark of a subject matter as it was, it lightened the mood. Sometimes you have to find the humor.

Later in the morning, we received a call from Father Alan, the priest we had hoped could perform the funeral service. He was back from retreat and we arranged to meet the following week. Whenever Mom's phone rang in the recent days, it could make me sad. I expected Dad's contact to pop up because he called various times throughout the day. She had the same ringtone for all of her calls; a soothing French song titled "La Vie en Rose," which Mom purchased after our family trip to Paris. Instead of Dad, the calls had been from people who wanted to express their condolences and hear all about the situation.

My uncle, Anthony, flew down from the Pacific Northwest and planned to stay with us through most of July. I hadn't seen him in a few years, so it was nice to be able to spend time with him. Mom had always been close to her brother, she even selected him to be my godfather. Mom's parents had owned our house before she and Dad purchased it, so he got to stay in his old bedroom. Our house felt livelier once Anthony arrived that afternoon.

He was knowledgeable on financial situations from the many years of doing insurance and workers compensation. He offered to accompany us to attorney meetings. We had a few meetings scheduled per week, as there was much to sort through regarding the business and estate. Sitting through some of the meetings over the past week made me feel as if I had aged twenty years. I had learned of different types of business licenses, estate planning, and the importance of creating a will.

The meetings were urgent and very involved because of the mess Dad's life had been. It was an odd blessing in disguise that we were forced to dedicate our days to focusing on the business instead of being allowed to stay home depressed all day.

More relatives from out of state had begun arriving. My cousins Bob, Kristen, and their daughter, Eve, spent the afternoon at our house. I appreciated being able to play with Eve. Young children are a great distraction because they are innocent during hard times. Having one person smiling, enjoying interacting with everyone there, helped me have relief during a very hard time. We played games and took crazy pictures on my phone.

It was hard to keep track of everyone arriving at our home, but I welcomed any diversion from my reality, which was easily possible. There was always someone over as a comforting presence. Rita corresponded with my friends to make sure I always had someone over while Peter was at work. I used to love being alone, but now I hated it. I imagined that it would feel lonely with no one around.

I stopped back to think about how generous people had been the past week. My hairstylist did our hair for free. Friends and family who were out of town offered their homes as get-aways; some even paid for a few vacations. People made us more food than we could eat.

Our dog groomer did baths for no charge, and we got offers from friends to watch our dogs if we were gone overnight. Rita and Callie came over and walked them for us when we were too busy; Callie even trained our stubborn puppy. The list went on and on.

People offered to alleviate our burdens in any way that they could. The generosity shown to us made me cry. Everyone went above and beyond with their help. There is so much kindness in the world which I learned of and experienced first-hand.

Anna Cambria

July 15, 2016

"But seek first the kingdom of God and his righteousness, and all these things will be added to you" (Matthew 6:33). It was easy to place blame on God: How could I believe in a God who would let this happen? Faith, however, was what got me through the loss. I couldn't miraculously have my father back, instead, I asked for the ability to move forward; God doesn't give you anything you can't handle.

Many were praying for us, and their prayers for strength were working. We needed it more than ever. Two women from our parish came over in the morning to give us a gift. I stayed in my room, sleeping in late, because I didn't feel up to socializing. I could hardly hear their conversation, but it sounded like they were giving us personalized prayer quilts. During the end of some Masses, people bring up quilts for a priest to bless. They are given out to people facing difficult times or if they are very ill. It never occurred to me that I would be one of those people to receive one.

After their brief visit, Mom came into my room and placed my quilt at the end of my bed. It had a green, pink, and yellow pattern. Each large patch had a pink string attached to its center. When the quilts were being crafted, as each of those strings was tied, a prayer was said. It was a thoughtful gesture. I kept it next to me for comfort every night.

It was crazy how quickly word spread. Not knowing what people were saying hurt; gossip was out of my control. I wanted everyone to come to us and hear the real story instead of hearing it secondhand. When people face hardships, others tend to speculate and worry, but we told them we were doing well. There was a certain line, however, a lot of people crossed.

Curiosity got the best of people, so we got asked personal questions about finances. "Are you going to move?" "How are you going to afford to continue living here?" "How much is the debt?" "Will you have to get rid of the dogs since they're an extra expense?" Many beat around the bush. Others blatantly asked questions. There were some who suggested we sell our house right away and move. It made me mad because it only added to my stress.

Since Mom and I were not employed during the summer, we could be with each other every step of the way; it was a blessing, but some didn't see it that way. A lot of people bombarded us with questions about what we were planning on doing for work. "Shouldn't you be looking for a job right now?" they harshly asked. When we spoke about finding something down the road that was part-time, they would respond, "Will that be enough pay though?" People were making assumptions. My greatest annoyance was the unwarranted advice from those who haven't gone through personal loss: "Work would get your mind off of this." There was no way Mom and I were in the right mindset to get a new job. Nothing could get our mind off this tragedy. I would nod and say "OK, thank you."

My current job was to be a detective, finding and connecting clues of my father's business. His associates were trying to find the root of the problem. Everyone wanted to know if this business had a chance to be saved and if there were designs on how to build prototypes. I went through a dozen thumb drives, searching through every folder. I was also hoping to find evidence from the documents saved to a Dropbox folder the same morning Dad passed.

He saved files that morning for a reason. He must have thought we would need those because they'd be important to the future of the company. Mom speculated that Dad went somewhere with Wi-Fi, possibly his old office or to a coffee shop, to send those to his Dropbox. There was no easy way to find out where he went, but it wasn't his new workplace.

The documents on his laptop, from 2008 through 2013, highlighted the best years of the business. The documents were for Dad's, at the time, "new inventions." I didn't want to look at them, they would make me long for the past, and there was no time for that. I numbed myself to the emotions and continued sifting through documents.

One of the most difficult things I had to do was delete Dad's LinkedIn profile. His profile picture had been taken at the height of his career. He looked so happy. All the proud comments he wrote on my LinkedIn posts were gone with the click of a button. I would never be able to look at his profile again nor read the words of praise he gave me on my accomplishments; people told me that he was the proudest father when it came to bragging about me.

Deleting the account was strange. It almost seemed necessary to keep it in case he needed it in the future. Luckily, he didn't have any other social media accounts or else it would have pained me more. Deleting his profile seemed representative of us moving on. His picture, in particular, was what made me the saddest. He was happy and healthy. His smile was genuine and he was proud of himself. After, I went and laid down on my bed and began sobbing.

It wasn't just his profile picture, any old pictures of Dad would make me cry. I began glancing over his face in pictures, making an effort to avoid looking at my own father. Sometimes, it wasn't only photos; I had to put his phone and laptop out of sight. They reminded me of the times when he would ask me for help with figuring out certain programs or apps on them. Who would have thought I'd miss playing technical support around the house.

All the Internet search history had been erased on Dad's computer. I was surprised that Dad knew how to erase all the data. He did not want us to see what he had been looking up. I originally wanted to know what he was searching because the history might contain clues. Perhaps it was for the better, it may have made me more depressed.

A sense of morbid curiosity hit me. I grabbed my phone, put it on private browsing mode to prevent a record of my search history being generated, and searched "How to commit suicide." The results disgusted me. There were actual websites instructing people how to kill themselves. Instead of clicking links, I put them out of my sight immediately. It is unbelievable that those websites are so accessible.

July 16, 2016

Taking multiple naps throughout the day had become a routine. I was tired all the time and worried that would continue for months to come. I dreaded the day of the funeral, yet looked forward to it. It would mark the beginning of moving towards healing. I hoped time would pass quickly from the many things we had to do.

There was no way I would sit around all day and be dejected. I wanted to live my life but the burdens remained: the funeral, the business, and no longer having Dad in my life. I could find memories of Dad in everything, even simply driving. I would pass a restaurant we frequented or a song he liked would come on the radio. He loved music. When I was young, he would sit on the floor, next to my bed, and play the guitar to help put me to sleep at night. His guitar remained in our house, but out of sight; it was a big part of him for a long time.

The smallest, seemingly insignificant connections, would spark powerful reactions. In my garage, I walked by a science textbook, and it made me burst out in tears. When I was in high school, Dad bought a "home science experiment kit" for me to do with friends, but it never interested me as a teenager. It remained unopened until we donated it years ago. I always felt guilty about it because Dad bought it for me and I never used it, even when he suggested it when friends were over. Seeing that textbook with similar packaging caused guilt and sadness to completely overwhelm me.

I had been suffering from an immense amount of guilt. I worried that I didn't spend enough time with Dad in the past, especially during the two weeks after his suicide attempt. It pained me to think he could have assumed I didn't care enough to have him around or, that if he did die, it "wouldn't affect me." The thought of no longer having a father haunted me during those weeks, but I couldn't be around him when he devastated my life, while acting like everything was fine. Dad was under extreme pressure and I wasn't there for him.

July 17, 2016

We visited the mausoleum where we had previously attended Mass on July 8th. This time, we had to pick out a location for future visitations of the urn. Our cousins, Michael and Leah, accompanied us. Their continued presence was comforting.

The office was located on the same grounds as the mausoleum, surrounded by acres of grass with thousands of burial sites; some tombstones dated back to the late 1800s. I had gone here many times with Mom to visit my grandparents' crypts but it would be different from this day forth. We walked into the office and were directed to a room where we would discuss locations and pricing. Sitting inside an air-conditioned building felt refreshing from the scorching sun.

A man walked through the door, holding a handout of the various locations available at the mausoleum. There were choices for indoor or outdoor niches. We decided an indoor location would be best because the weather wouldn't damage its quality. It was amazing how many places were already occupied or reserved in such a vast facility. The cemetery already seemed filled from corner to corner. Despite this, the man assured us that plenty of space was still available.

We settled on a two-foot by two-foot space on a

locked shelf. The urn would be encased in glass where it, and any mementos, would be visible to those who would walk by. I had passed by the urn housing many times; it was in a beautiful area. The mausoleum was large, almost labyrinth-like in its layout, and similar looking throughout. This area, however, was easy to navigate to.

Admittedly, I forgot the conversations we had inside the office with the manager. My memory developed a habit of randomly forgetting to hit the record button. I am unsure if it was because some moments were too emotionally difficult to accept, if I was mentally exhausted, or if my mind wandered to happier places. Perhaps it was a combination of all three. What I did remember was leaving to head up to the mausoleum, which would have been a long walk away from the office.

The temperature had remained close to a hundred degrees for the entire month. It would have been unbearable to walk that far distance, so we drove over instead. We all rode in the man's car, which was a very large Town Car from the 1970s. The interior of it was comically outdated with red leather seats and a felt roof. It was well preserved though.

When we pulled up to the mausoleum entrance, the place had a whole different feel now. It was always a dismal place to go to, but this time, it felt more real. The idea that the dead were stored within the granite walls of the mausoleum had always unfazed me. Now, the concept hit me with force. My father's physical remains would spend eternity here.

Mom, my cousins, and I walked over to the glass encasings. The man showed us the end spot we had chosen, and we confirmed our decision. By being on the corner, it was visible from the side as well as the front. It was at eye level, so items placed inside could easily be viewed. They, of course, asked my mom if she wanted to purchase a larger niche in order for them to be together. As a group, we decided to get him an individual niche, and not pressure Mom to think of that. "You're still so young," Leah said.

July 18, 2016

Mom and I went to the parish office to meet with Father Alan. His office was like any other, only with many crosses displayed. I stayed quiet, any word I said would undoubtedly bring tears. Mom told the whole story again, the same way she had the past week. Each time it felt unreal.

We were there to pick out the readings and learn the details of the Mass. I didn't care what readings we chose, it had been too hard to look up verses and Psalms pertaining to death. Opening up a Bible to a random page, choosing whatever passage stuck out, seemed more desirable. We picked a day for the funeral, July 22nd, which was exactly two weeks after Dad's death. Coincidentally, a year ago on that very same day, we had a backyard birthday party for me and a cousin. We had friends and family over as well as a bounce house (who says they are only for little kids). We would be having people over again on that day, though under terrible circumstances.

My parents were married at the same church that the funeral service was to be performed. I was thinking about how I'd rather be there planning a wedding Mass than a funeral Mass. They both have a similar order, although the mood of the room is the primary differentiator. Initially, I didn't want to have a service. It would be especially hard to sit through a funeral for my father when the circumstances were as horrible as this. Many of the attendees in the room, including myself, would be torn between being upset about his passing and feeling angry he took his own life. Mom reassured me it is important to have a service. There were a lot of people who wanted to pay their final respects.

Dad's friend, Andy, wanted to give a eulogy as a form of closure. I wouldn't have the strength to talk in front of everyone, but I respected Andy for having the courage to find peace in his own way. Hearing him talk about Dad was going to be difficult. We asked Father Alan if it would be OK to incorporate him at the end of the Mass. To be granted permission, Father Alan requested that Andy mention Dad's faith in his writings of the eulogy.

Suicide is a tricky topic. It's considered a "grave sin" in our faith, which is a major sin that separates a person from God's grace. This left Mom with a lot of questions. She was worried that Dad couldn't have a Catholic funeral or be buried in a Catholic cemetery. Also, cremation was not always allowed because it isn't preserving the body; it was only in recent times that it became acceptable. Sometimes a body is in very poor condition and would be better if cremated, which was what we had to do.

Dad was a practicing Catholic who knew this was very wrong, but under the immense stress, he could not stand it to continue. His quality of life was diminished and, towards the end, kept saying he had sins and was a failure. Anguish and psychological problems caused him to not be in his right mind; such as what Sister Carol told us: it was a "mind attack." Mom and I were reassured that we were doing the right thing after talking to Father Alan. We thanked him and left.

On our way home, we made a stop at a store that specializes in Catholic gifts. We wanted to get prayer cards to give out at the funeral. I had no idea the store existed. It was filled with shelves of relics, colorful rosaries, crosses of all different sizes and materials, Sacrament pendants, the host used for Eucharist, and other items for any necessity.

As Mom and I looked around, a lady behind the counter came over to us. "Can I help you find anything?" she asked. Mom replied, "We needed prayer cards for my husband who recently passed away." She was a friendly person, but I caught the moment her smile turned from genuine to concerned. She sat us down and asked us how he passed away. The room turned gloomier before Mom even began to talk. Once again, she told a summarized version of the event.

The lady looked devastated by what she had heard. She acted very sympathetic towards us; I had grown accustomed to these reactions. She then handed us a book filled with Bible verses that we could choose to put on the back of the prayer cards. We narrowed it down to one choice, Prayer of St. Francis. It's a very common prayer used for funerals or during Masses.

As we were about to finalize the decision, Mom spotted a prayer card right next to her. Out of curiosity, she read it. It fit our situation perfectly, and was titled "I am Free." Some excerpts greatly stood out:

"Don't grieve for me, for now I am free"
"I could not stay another day To laugh to love, to work, or play"
"If my parting has left a void, Then fill it with remembering joy"
"My life's been full, I've savored much, Good friends, good times, a loved one's touch"
"Perhaps my time seemed all too brief, Don't lengthen it now with undue grief"
"God wanted me now – He set me free."

While I missed my father dearly, I could understand that he is now free. Free from the pressure brought on by the business, as well as from all of his other demons that haunted him throughout his life. He no longer has the excruciating stress.

For the front of the prayer card, we chose the image of St. Francis of Assisi, the patron saint of animals and nature. In the image, St. Francis is out in a field, near a tree. He is surrounded by birds and it appears as if he is talking to them. Dad loved being in nature, hearing the birds chirping from the trees and seeing the bunnies and lizards crossing his paths on hikes. That was his serenity.

Back at home, I created the pamphlets for the funeral Mass. It felt like an unusually grim class project from an off-beat graphic design professor, not a pamphlet for my father's actual funeral. I thought about the time in college, four years ago, when my friend, Natalie, and I took a math class. There were over 200 students in it, so the professor didn't know us personally. We were going on vacation but had a major test scheduled during the time we would be gone. Death or illness was the only excusable way to miss it. We made a funeral pamphlet for a made-up family friend, so we could be excused to make up the test at a different time.

The teaching assistant bought the lie easily, even though I felt slightly regretful because he was a nice man. This time, it wasn't something I could laugh about later. This pamphlet was the real thing. Staring at Dad's picture on the front page of the pamphlet was unnerving. Mom had chosen the portrait, a picture of him taken the day of their wedding 33 years ago. He was 25 years old and looked handsome in his suit. To most, Dad had not been remembered as the sweet, happy man. His legacy had turned from brilliant inventor to the "bad guy." Seeing an end date to my own father's life below his image was disheartening. He would no longer be there for the remainder of the many years left of my life.

The man in the picture was the fun father at my birthday parties, the creative one who built set designs for plays I was in, the creator of the coolest forts and swing sets in our backyard, and the most caring and kind person. When I was growing up, our backyard was transformed into a playground because of his creativity. He spoiled me and planned to spoil my kids too. He was excited for the milestone when he and Mom would be "cool grandparents" to my children. Dad never talked negatively about the future and, if anything, he was looking forward to it.

Everyone used to say that I was lucky to have such a family-oriented father. Now, it made me tear up whenever people told me that he loved me more than anything. It made me wish that I reciprocated that love more while he was alive. I was not the perfect daughter as he had been the perfect father. I took everything he did for me for granted. He made me feel like the most loved daughter in the world. It was hard to think of that when I had resentment towards him for devastating me.

I fluctuated between wishing to see Dad again and being mad at him forever. Seeing his face one more time could make me sad or angry. He was the father I love, but he left Mom after she had been with him through life's journey. They planned on retiring and traveling together. An exciting future of travel and grandkids was not enough for him to stick around. None of us knew the full extent of his suffering, but now everyone appeared upset with him.

July 21, 2016

The following day was not only the funeral, but it was also the day that I could begin anew. I had spent every night, for the past two weeks, crying. God knows how many tissues I used. Random things could make me cry, but I was strong at other times. When I was fine and happy, I felt guilty. From all of the looks of sympathy, I assumed I was supposed to always feel despondent. People never knew exactly how to approach me or what to say.

I began to think about all the visits we had from friends and family the past month, people were over from dawn till dusk. The financial and moral support we received from everyone was a blessing. The thought of the help slowly fading out crossed my mind. Most would move on with their lives, which would make me feel alone. We would always have help from those close to us, such as Peter, Rita, Jessica's family, and my cousins, but it was still worrisome. My goal was to take one day at a time.

I did as much as I could to prepare for the following morning. My cousin, Kathy, washed and styled my hair; it would be one less thing to worry about doing in the morning. I selected my clothes to avoid the stress of picking out an appropriate outfit. The funeral was set to begin at 10am. I had to be ready.

Anna Cambria

July 22, 2016 – 8:30 am

After putting on my black pencil skirt and teal patterned top, I stared into the full length mirror in my room; I was dressed for my father's funeral. I did not want the people who would attend to see me cry, so I brought sunglasses and wore waterproof mascara. There was, roughly, half a box of tissues stuffed into my small purse.

Mom went with Anthony, Michael, and Leah in the morning to retrieve the urn. Going with them seemed to be an unnecessary burden, so I drove to the church separately with Peter. The drive over was quiet; my stomach was in knots, my hands sweaty. We picked up water bottles on the way because my mouth was already dry. My past worries all seemed trivial compared to this day.

Walking through the church doors an hour before the Mass was scheduled to start, I was surprised how many family members were already there. They were setting up pictures and flowers in front of the altar. Arriving at an empty church would have been much more difficult; love was already surrounding me, and it felt peaceful.

We had a guest book that attendees could use to sign and leave a message if they chose. I have been to funerals in the past where people lined up to talk to the family after, but I was glad Mom agreed that we didn't have to do that. We made this choice for a few reasons: the number of guests, the limited time we had, and it would be too difficult to see the tears. Most knew to respect our distance; I would not be able to properly converse.

Seeing those that I had already talked to in the past two weeks was easier for me than talking to new people; we had already passed the initial conversation. That conversation was always the most draining; no one knew how to properly express their grief and the emotions were raw. I would eventually have to talk to everyone who came to Mass, but today was not that day.

Peter and I sat in a pew in front of the church. Shortly after, Michael, Leah, Anthony, and Mom entered. They passed us in silence as they walked towards the altar. Michael was holding the urn, it was no longer a picture on the TV screen in the mortuary. Inside of that sand-colored, marble urn was what was left of Dad's body. Mom had held the urn on her lap during the entire car ride from the mortuary to the church. I couldn't imagine what that must have been like to hold your husband's remains.

Michael placed the urn on a table, in front of the altar, beside a framed picture of Dad. The black frame was engraved with Dad's name, his birth and death date, and a short inscription reading: "Beloved Husband and Father." The picture itself was taken by Mom at the top of a mountain that the three of us loved to hike. It was a place Dad used to go to clear his mind, as well as to get a great workout in. Also on the table was a wooden plaque, given to us by Michael and Leah a few days ago. On it, there were carvings of a tree with footprints leading to a mountain range. A beautiful passage was etched into the wood:

"Climb the mountains and get their good tidings. Nature's peace will flow into you as sunshine flows into trees. The winds will blow their own freshness into you, and the storms their energy, while care will drop away from you like the leaves of Autumn" -John Muir

"Thank you for walking through our lives. The footprints you left behind will always be remembered and loved."

The urn was in the center of the table, with the framed photograph to the left and the engraved plaque to the right. It was a difficult moment to witness the table being arranged, so I sat in the pew instead of getting up to help. Just a month before, I wouldn't have imagined I'd see a memorial of Dad there. Even though it had already been two weeks, it didn't seem that he was permanently gone; his actions still remained unbelievable.

I could sense movement in the background as more people began entering the church. The main door to the church is located in the back and there are two side doors in the center of each side. I was tempted to turn around to see who had come, but I didn't want to make contact with anyone. My eyes were locked forward, everyone was quiet and respectful not to approach us.

I experienced the sorrow of everyone there. Each person who attended was impacted by Dad's death in some way, a death that was preventable and senseless. Just hearing that someone committed suicide can horrify even an acquaintance. It was still embarrassing for me due to having the stigma that my father committed suicide. He had been thought of differently now, so I believed that my family didn't have the same, good image it always had. Everyone from my elementary school knew, and I'm sure most of my high school classmates found out as well. The classmates who didn't know my father personally would have a flawed image of him.

Mom sat down next to me in the pew. Our tissues and water bottles were accessible to the both of us. I was lucky to have an amazing mom and boyfriend sitting on either side of me. I prayed that I wouldn't cry during the funeral. If the attendants saw me distraught, it would only make the service harder to bear.

The church was filled to capacity with those who came to pay their respects; the majority of them had never been to the church before. It was uplifting to be surrounded by people I care about, and who cared for my father. Others in attendance, the members of our parish, never knew Dad personally but came to support his friends and family. I found myself wishing I was strong enough to personally go around to thank each person who attended, but it would have been too difficult to speak to anyone. We would go forward with our plan to follow Father Alan out of the church after the service, then walk straight to our cars to head over to the mausoleum.

The choir sang "Be not Afraid" to begin the Mass at 10am: "You shall cross the barren desert, but you shall not die of thirst. You shall wander far in safety though you do not know the way. You shall speak your words in foreign lands and all will understand. You shall see the face of God and live." It is often used for funerals at a Catholic church.

Father Alan walked down the aisle, followed by a pair of fellow pastors who joined to preside over the Mass. One was from the church while the other from the parish where I went to elementary school. Mom had worked at my elementary school for fourteen years but wanted the funeral to be at the church where they had been married.

Once the service began, I braced for the readings and words that were going to be said about Dad. I wanted to tune it all out. Even though this was a funeral Mass dedicated to my own father, I was waiting for him to arrive and sit down next to us.

Sounds of sniffles echoed throughout the church. My heart ached for Grandma. She was sitting a row diagonal to me with her head down. Her eyes were closed as she held a tissue up to her nose. She had now outlived two of her children. I returned my gaze forward, towards the three priests, and kept my eyes away from the urn.

It was a beautiful service. The singers' voices were

angelic and two of my cousins did Bible readings. They kindly offered to stand in place for Mom and I. Being up on the altar, speaking, would have been too difficult. Andy gave his eulogy at the end of the Mass. It choked me up when he mentioned how proud Dad was of me. Everyone had been telling me how much Dad loved and talked about me. I had lost that support and hadn't been able to sense his presence. Because of my anger, I tried hard not to roll my eyes whenever someone told me, "Your dad is here in spirit watching over you. He wants you to be happy." The only way he could've made me happy was if he was still here. Today, however, I felt Dad for the first time. He was watching and listening to his friends and family.

When the service concluded, close family members, Mom, Peter, and I walked out behind the priests. Mom and I led the way, looking down with our sunglasses on to avoid eye contact. Once we exited the church, we thanked Father Alan and the other priests; they understood we wanted to leave right away. Father Alan was going to join us at the mausoleum after talking to the guests for us.

When I got in Peter's car, I looked out across the parking lot to see the people who were beginning to leave the church. The first to exit were some I had never seen before. I figured that I could look in the guest book later to see who was there. Regardless of if I knew them personally or not, everyone's attendance meant so much to me. They cared for my father and took time out of their day to attend, most missing work for the first part of the day.

Mom, Anthony, Michael, and Leah rode together to the mausoleum with the urn. It was a 20-minute drive, so we departed immediately. As we drove away, and the church disappeared from view, I breathed a sigh of relief. The moment of ease was temporary; although the funeral was over, the hardest part was to come.

July 22, 2016 – 12:00 pm

About 15 of us went to the mausoleum for the interment. Grandma was too upset to come, so she was taken home by my cousins Keith and Sofia. Peter and I were the first to arrive. We had some time before, so I walked around the beautiful mausoleum and took Peter to my maternal grandparents' crypts. Each time Mom and I go to the mausoleum, we visit them. I never met my grandfather, and my grandmother died a few weeks after I was born. We usually light two candles as a dedication to them. Once a year, we put up a new arrangement of artificial flowers to last all year. My grandparents are laid to rest at the top level of the rows of crypts, so it's always a challenge putting flowers up. I have to grab a reacher that can grasp onto the two brown plastic flower cups and hope that they don't come falling down.

After wandering, we returned to the front of the mausoleum to see other family starting to arrive. I went over to the entrance to greet and guide them to where the short service was to be held. A row of metal chairs was set up for us in front of the wall of the glass niches. Mom, Dad's sister, and I sat directly in the middle. There weren't enough chairs for everyone, so some stood behind us.

The niche, usually locked, was open. The urn was placed inside next to the framed picture of Dad that was at the service. There was complete silence as we sat, waiting for Father Alan to join us. After a minute went by, Mom said, "[My husband] wouldn't have liked this silence. If he was here, he'd have to make a joke or start talking." We all chuckled. The mood lightened a shade. It was true; he always had to say something to avoid any awkward silence. I thought back to times when Dad would always insist on making conversation with every cab or bus driver, even when it was clear that the driver was a quiet guy.

A few minutes later, Father Alan joined and began the interment. He read a few passages from the Bible and blessed everything we had in the niche with holy water. While trying to distract my mind from what was going on in front of me, a thought crossed my mind: I was almost free. When this ceremony was over, I would be able to move on with my life.

After the final blessing, everyone walked away to allow Mom and me privacy. It was time to pay our final respects. Inside, we placed Dad's worn prayer book, a laminated handwritten note about self-help that he always kept in his wallet, a St. Christopher medal, and a memento from his favorite place, Disneyland. That was one of the hardest parts of the day. We were face to face with his urn. It was our final goodbye. When we were finished, a man who worked at the mausoleum closed and sealed the niche as Mom and I walked away.

July 22, 2016 – 1:45 pm

As we arrived back at our house for the reception, we saw our street packed with cars. There were over twenty friends and family who were already there, waiting for the rest of us to arrive. It was a mini-reunion for both sides of the family; they hadn't been under the same roof in years. I had only wished it was under better circumstances, but everyone wanted to be there. It was special for Mom to have her brothers Paul, John, and Anthony there. I couldn't help but expect Dad to be there as his usual social self, chatting and making people laugh. I knew, however, he was there in spirit.

It was the hottest day of the month so far, and our air conditioning was still not working well. Our house became crowded; more bodies meant more body heat in the rooms. The day had already been filled with mourning, the oppressive temperature only made matters worse. Everyone stayed indoors or huddled outside next to the fans.

We had Mexican food catered. The spread of food was beautiful. A buffet of tacos, rice, beans, enchiladas, salads, and more were set up in our backyard under a covered tent. A man from the restaurant was serving food; he must have felt miserable standing out in the heat while wearing black clothes. I tried my best to enjoy the food, but I had no appetite. Peter, Rita, Callie, and I sat on the couch in the living room. The material on the couch was microfiber, so it didn't help with cooling us down. Drinking a cold beverage or sitting near a fan still wasn't enough.

My room, with the door closed and no foot traffic, had managed to cool down unlike the other rooms. A few of us sought refuge there, with the ceiling fan on maximum speed; it once again became my place of escape. We had a normal conversation while hanging out, like any you would expect to overhear at a regular party. Nothing sad was mentioned, and I appreciated that. I did not want to talk about my father, despite being at a funeral reception for him. Mom, however, couldn't have a conversation that wasn't about Dad. Everyone was asking questions, wanting to know about the debts and what would become of Dad's business. She didn't even have answers to that yet.

A few more started joining us in my small room once they noticed that it was cooler in there. Another reason they came was to talk to me about my recent accomplishment: earning my bachelor's degree. I thought everyone had forgotten about it since this summer was based around my father. Today was the mark to begin creating my happy life again.

After such a busy day, I was exhausted and craved sleep. The stress of planning a funeral, with the anticipation of the day itself looming over me, was gone. I could rebuild my life. Mom had helped me handle this tough journey. She was devastated and shocked, I'm sure she had many days wanting to collapse and stay in bed, but she pressed ahead. I simply followed the steps she had already taken for us. I had been blessed with the strongest mother as my support.

July 25, 2016

Days had passed since the funeral. Everything had begun to calm down. People backed away, the phone didn't ring as often, and cards and flowers stopped arriving. Most had flown home but Uncle Anthony stayed for a few more days. His knowledge had helped Mom when her attention became solely on our financial problems and uncertain future.

She had to check our PO Box a few times a week. We forwarded all of Dad's work mail to it after he moved out of the office days before his death. The credit card companies and IRS notifications had been frequent, making every trip to the mailbox dreadful. What would we discover about our financial situation today? Seeing credit card bills with overdue charges and bills from Dad's attorneys added to the anxiety. Mom feared that we were going to be liable for these, even when we did not have previous knowledge of anything.

Things around our house started to go awry as well. Lights went out in the yard, water fountains stopped working, and our sprinkler system failed to properly function. When one thing was fixed, something else would break. We were fortunate to have help from Jessica's and Michael's family when it came to fixing problems or doing various chores around the house. They wanted to alleviate our workload and give us the breathing room we needed to stabilize ourselves. I still felt dependent on people.

Relationships became important to me; they were greatly strengthened. I decided to be a better friend, and started going through my phone contact list, pressing on names of old friends I hadn't spoken to in a while. I sent out a few messages, asking them if they wanted to grab dinner. It was exciting conversing with them again and arranging a time to get together.

It was a drastic change from earlier in the month; I never wanted to make plans. Because of the stress, I easily got mad at someone for the smallest things or if I didn't get my way. Even though I was aware of this issue, it was hard to correct. My misplaced anger could have hurt my friendships. Another issue was that I couldn't guarantee hanging out because I might end up bailing on them. My mood changed hour to hour, so I never knew what to feel. Peter, Rita, and Callie were the only ones who treated me as a friend, not someone to be treated with pity.

Once I could pass the initial embarrassment, I would be more comfortable hanging out with others. It had been hard seeing someone that I hadn't talked to since Dad's death. Whenever we met up, their faces changed right away. It was like they were witnessing the saddest moment they had ever seen. People were cautious, some even avoided Mom and me as much as they could. That was why I thought I would be the one to reach out now that more time had passed.

July 26, 2016

After weeks of waiting, we finally received the California Highway Patrol report: a detailed explanation of what occurred the morning of July 8th. It said that an officer pulled up behind Dad's parked car, which was at the center of the bridge. The officer intended to do a welfare check because he saw that someone was in the car; the engine was still running. Before he could reach the car, Dad ran out and leaped over the side of the 450-foot tall bridge.

Dad could have either waited for someone to come so there would be a witness, or, once he saw the police car pull up, he had to hurry and do it. With the officer as a witness, there wasn't a need for an investigation. The officer opened the car door to see if there was anything important. The same suicide note was on the passenger seat.

Mom had read the new note, weeks ago, when we obtained the possessions that were inside the car. This time Dad had added, "I'm so sorry again" to the end of it. Apologizing again for committing suicide was a joke to me. Those mild words are used after accidentally stepping on someone's foot or for children to say if they get mad at someone on the playground, not for knowing they were going to devastate the rest of someone's life.

Although I didn't witness anything, my mind had created an image of what everything would have looked or been like. I saw Dad's car parked on a bridge that spanned the space high up between two mountains. Images of Dad fleeing the car, viewing the ground far below, with a grim look on his face, were in my mind. I wondered how witnessing that tragedy impacted the officer; he was the last one to see my father alive.

July 27-28, 2016

When looking for the small signs in life, I began to see Dad was there, watching out for me. I believe that those who are deceased can send signs letting loved ones on Earth know that they are with us in spirit. It can be encountering someone, even briefly, who can offer you hope.

Mom and I met an amazing woman who volunteered at a wildlife rescue organization. It was no coincidence; she was placed in our lives for a reason. What was even more incredible was that this event was seemingly foretold on the image of the St. Francis prayer cards from the funeral.

It all started when Mom was watering the plants in the afternoon. Out of the corner of her eye, she saw something moving. A few feet away from her were two baby birds, blending in with the dirt on the ground. They were unable to fly or walk. Their nest had fallen out of a tree in our yard. It was destroyed, but the babies survived.

Mom called me to come out to the yard so I could see. They were vulnerable; all they could do was stare back at us. We weren't sure what actions to take, but we decided the best option would be to put them back in the tree. I placed the baby birds, and what was left of the nest, inside of a small, white basket. The basket couldn't fit in the location that they were near previously, so I hung it by a wire on a different branch. The babies were silent, which made me fear that the parents wouldn't be able to locate them.

Getting the birds off of my mind was impossible. I worried about them throughout the night, even going to check on them a few times. With my flashlight in hand, I walked outside in my pajamas, peeking inside the basket. Their eyes were open, still looking around. I would feel at fault if they didn't make it through the night. It depressed me to think that they didn't have anyone to take care of them; their parents could have abandoned them.

Soon after waking up the next morning, I rushed out to the yard. Seeing both birds slightly moving around made me overjoyed that they survived, yet I didn't know the last time they had eaten. Something had to be done. It became a race against time. I called our local veterinarian and was directed to a wildlife non-profit near our home. According to the non-profit's website, they were opening in a half hour.

Mom unhooked the basket from our tree. I secured it in-between my legs for the car ride over, frequently glancing down at them out of concern. They looked weak and were opening their mouths in what I guessed to be a sign of hunger. The nest was dirty from all the bird droppings scattered about. It looked like one had a hurt wing. The wing was positioned uncomfortably, but I didn't touch it out of fear that I could cause damage to it. The other was already attempting to fly out of the basket.

The wildlife organization was in an industrial park. A man was also dropping off a bird. I was surprised to see someone else; it had never before crossed my mind about how needed an organization like this is. In the lobby of the building, cages were available for overnight drop-offs of animals. About twenty cages of all different sizes were set up, but none held animals. I wondered if any animals were in there before the organization opened this morning.

Behind the front desk was a wide variety of colorful, wild birds; it was very noisy. A volunteer determined that our birds were a type of finch. She was able to take and feed them through a syringe. I was grateful that they could finally eat food. We left the birds with them, but they asked for our contact information to keep us updated on their condition.

We thanked the volunteers and headed home. I had no knowledge that this organization so close to us existed. Incredible individuals work there for no pay, just out of the kindness of their hearts. Mom and I drove home feeling more comfortable that the birds were in good hands. I felt proud of the small part that we did for helping the helpless.

Only a few hours later, we received a call from the organization. They informed us that someone would be on the way to help put the birds back in a new nest. Using a recorded bird call of the same species would attract the parents to the babies. After hanging up, Mom and I were skeptical about the method; the parents seemed long gone.

A woman from the organization arrived, her car was filled with birds that she planned on releasing into the wild later in the day. She introduced herself as Silvia. Silvia seemed to be in her 60s and had long, curly brown hair. After brief introductions, she asked if she could bring the birds into our house, as the car would quickly grow hot in the July heat.

We carried ten small cages into our house. It was comical how many wild birds were on the chairs by our kitchen table. A bright red colored bird was especially vocal, choosing to express its opinions in loud and constant chirps. Our dogs, forced to be outside by our unexpected guests, peered in fascination through the glass door.

With the birds safely indoors, Silvia walked out with the finches. It was cute to see them again. They were now in a makeshift nest inside a strawberry basket. She asked us where the nest fell out of and tied the strawberry basket on a branch in the area. Then she retrieved a small, black speaker box from her car and began playing the bird call recording. She wandered around the yard, holding up the speaker box. It only took a few minutes until we saw a bird flutter by, shortly followed by a second one. I was surprised to see these birds. They must have remained hidden the entire time, unable to locate their babies after their nest had been moved. It was amazing to witness both parents coming back for them. The babies were finally being taken care of again. We could hear them all happily chirping.

Silvia returned inside our house to retrieve the other birds in the kitchen. She noticed the funeral flowers and the pictures of Dad. She asked us who had passed away. While talking, we learned that Silvia had known many loved ones who attempted or committed suicide. It was tragic enough to deal with one person I loved commit suicide, but knowing multiple people who did seemed unimaginable. We asked her why she volunteers at the rescue and how she has been able to get through such hardships. "You heal by helping others," she said. That saying stuck with me, maybe that was why those baby birds came into our lives. It felt satisfying to save two innocent animals that day.

Sometimes, the people who have gone through the hardest situations are the ones who want to help others the most. Silvia had her share of heartaches but she cared for others to help herself heal. Finally meeting someone else who had been through a similar situation made me feel that I wasn't alone. She had been able to live her life well through her good deeds. I realized that I could get through this, it would just take time.

Comfort was felt that day. Because of her, hope was instilled in me. Dad would have been touched by her caring for us and the animals. She gave us both long hugs and words of encouragement before she left. Having been through it too, she knew how to talk to us and what to say. Silvia was placed in our lives for a reason, the timing wasn't a coincidence.

July 31, 2016

This July had been the most difficult month of my life, and it was now over. What made July even harder was that my birthday fell at the end of it. I was nowhere near excited for the day. My parents always made each birthday special for me, but this year, it didn't feel like a time to celebrate. On the morning of my 23rd birthday, a few days prior, there was a noticeable absence.

It was a dreary morning, but Mom helped push me through it. She wrote me a beautiful birthday card that I couldn't get through without tearing up and gave me a watch that her mother had worn. Despite the obvious void, I was going to try and enjoy my day without feeling guilty. That's why Mom didn't pressure me to attend Mass at the mausoleum with her on my birthday morning.

Mom took me to a sushi restaurant for lunch once she returned home. Getting out of the house helped me clear my head. I munched on California rolls as we avoided any conversation about Dad. He, in one way or another, had dominated most conversations over the last month. I only wanted positivity this day.

To keep the celebration going through the evening, Rita organized a birthday dinner for me. We went out with a group of friends to one of my favorite Mexican restaurants. We sat outside in an open patio area, the summer night was beautiful. The crowded restaurant was alive with conversation.

After dinner, we walked through the heart of downtown to take in the city life on the busy streets. People were out walking their dogs, going to restaurants, out with friends at bars, or simply enjoying the night air and bayside views. While looking for a place to fix our sweet tooth, we spotted a café with an array of desserts. We bought macaroons and cannoli. After carving out some room amongst the crowded tables, we listened to the live Italian music being played next door.

The night was flawless, but that's not why I cherished the evening; *I was treated normally*. I did not receive any looks of pity nor words of condolences. Everyone had a night filled with good memories and laughter. I had to remind myself not to feel guilty for going out. Looking at photos from that night reminded me of the fun we had while taking them. The laughter was genuine, the smiles sincere. Dad would have wanted me to enjoy my night; all he ever wanted was for me to be happy.

My goal for the month of August was to make myself my number one priority. It was a challenge to see a bright future, though, when I had to hear and tell the same story multiple times each day. However, it was good therapy in itself to not be afraid to talk about it. I could share my story easier, without choking up. In fact, I began to hope it was helping others. Suicide, and the discussion of it, holds a social stigma. Many who have never dealt with it don't openly discuss it, those who have are often ashamed to bring to light the issues they're facing. Conversation by conversation, I hoped to normalize it just a touch.

August 1, 2016

Although Anthony had flown home, we still had plenty of comfort from those who lived close by. A family friend of ours, Rose, was an amazing source to help us make sense of Dad's passing. We had known her for over ten years but, as of the past month, we grew even closer. She had a comforting approach, having experienced loss herself. She was also very strong in her faith. This was the first night that we were able to have one on one time with her. She brought over chicken tacos and salad for the three of us to enjoy.

We discussed the wonderful man Dad was, the one most of us failed to remember in the past weeks. I hadn't talked about that side of him lately; he had lost respect by many because his decision had hurt everyone. I fluctuated between hating the businessman but sad for my father who loved to play with me as a kid. He gave me the happiest childhood; my favorite part of the day was when he came home from work. Remembering how loved he made me feel helped us understand his pain of not being able to support his family.

Rose shared her thoughts on how a happy family man could succumb to this "illness." She saw Dad as the kind and caring man that he was. "He couldn't live with himself knowing he hurt so many people," she said, "He had a good conscience." That was exactly what I needed to hear. Dad felt overwhelmed with guilt. He became someone he never wanted to be in order to save the company and provide for his family. In the end, he convinced himself that everyone would hate him. They could think of him as a failure for not having success in the innovations that many had generously invested in.

Our conversations ranged from sad reminiscing to our favorite memories with great laughs. We enjoyed dinner and spoke of the bright future. Rose was one of the few people to have a clear head to discuss Dad's death with understanding instead of anger. She found peace in this situation for us. All I could think about the past month were the bad times. I did not even want him here "in spirit," directing me towards a successful future. Why would he want me to have a good life if he abandoned us? Rose helped change that mentality for Mom and me. We can't let someone's faults cause us to hate them, especially if we once loved them.

Rose gave me a gift basket and inside of it was a blue notebook with colorful butterflies on it. Butterflies symbolize the resurrection of those who have passed on, to show they are here looking out for us. I had noticed more butterflies fluttering around our home the past weeks.

I opened up the notebook and saw that there were quotes inside. One greatly spoke to me: "Forgiveness is a way of life that gradually transforms us from being helpless victims of our circumstances to being powerful and loving co-creators of our reality" (Robin Casarjian). We cannot be a victim of anger and hate for the rest of our lives, or else there is no room for love in our hearts. Yes, what Dad did could be labeled as incredibly selfish, but I will never know what was going on in his mind. I would have to forgive him at some point in order to accept my new life. Carrying the burden of being non-forgiving is only hurting myself.

Having Rose over distracted us from our chaotic

life. We had recently learned that the threats of lawsuits were no longer just threats. A trial was beginning between members of the board. The companies in heated arguments were furious and had enough. Each believed they owned the full rights to various products; one side refused to give the technology to the other, holding it "hostage." Mom was amongst the escalating turmoil and hoped she wouldn't have to testify. It would be torture to be forced to view faces of individuals who aided in her husband's misery.

There were a few people in the business, however, who focused on helping preserve Dad's legacy and cleaning up the disorder. Having good people surrounding us, who made it their sole intention to help, eased the burden considerably. The main one being Dad's long-time friend, Stan. Stan helped oversee business-related matters to relieve Mom of that stress. He wanted to see if it was possible to save all of the intellectual properties and companies that Dad had worked for most of his career.

We called him a saint for everything he did for Dad, his company, and us personally. Stan told us, "He wouldn't let me help him in life, so I will help him after death." No one could have done as much work to try to preserve a legacy as he did.

August 13, 2016

Michael, Leah, and their two sons, Cody and Mark, came over around 6am. They were going to help with a garage sale. Going through Dad's belongings over the past week was a huge task. Mom was strong and did most of it; I couldn't handle it. In the back of my mind was the flawed notion that we shouldn't throw away anything, that Dad would return and need his things.

His clothing sparked the most memories: baseball hats that he bought as souvenirs on our family vacations, his sunglasses that he wore every day, and his favorite t-shirts. Six months ago I bought him a hat from my college as a Christmas present, now it would be given to a stranger. It was important to keep some possessions of his, but we had to let go of most clothes and personal items; they only served as painful reminders. He owned hundreds of books. I kept a few on marketing and entrepreneurship. I inherited my love of reading and learning new information from Dad.

It seemed like each day that passed, the weather grew hotter and hotter. The day of the garage sale was no exception. Standing in the direct sun for even less than a minute caused our skin to burn, but we had to put everything outside. We stood in the shade of the trees for some relief. It was miserable for my hands to pick things up that had been in the direct sunlight. The enjoyable part of the day was the breakfast spread of bagels and donuts shared with family and friends who joined us throughout the morning.

People were coming over to us, holding up items, asking, "How much?" How do you price a ten-year-old jacket that your father wore weekly? No one who bought his possessions knew the story behind each one. Some probably assumed they were from my cousin, Michael, who was sitting outside with us. The anonymity was OK. You have to disconnect to do this.

Even after the garage sale, we had two large truckloads of unsold items to donate. Michael and Leah drove away with everything as I turned back to look at the sparse garage. It used to be filled to capacity from all of Dad's projects. Back in the 1990s, a camping trailer, designed and built entirely by Dad, had been parked in there. I loved going inside of it, sitting on the pull-out bed, wishing that we could go camping. A window was located on the roof where we would be able to look at the stars. We never ended up using the camper; he sold it a few years after completion.

Once everyone left in the afternoon, I went through the bins filled with my school work, throwing away anything that wasn't meaningful or important to me. Some of it dated back to my elementary school years. I stumbled across handwritten notes from Dad, saying how much he loved me. I wanted to throw all of them inside the trash bag out of spite, but I reluctantly kept a few. My better senses told me I'd regret it down the road.

The notes reminded me of the fun-loving father who made me the happiest little girl in the world each day. Often times, we would put on a CD and dance to songs. I would stand on his shoes while he held my arms. Even though he was tired from a long day, he still made time to play with his enthusiastic, five-year-old daughter.

I realize now that on the last night with Dad, when

we were playing video games, he was trying to create a lasting memory that I could cherish when he was gone. We were laughing and joking about the game. I had learned that suicidal people can suddenly become happy because they know their pain will soon be over. He was in a good mood that night. To me, it appeared that progress was being made in his recovery, but to him, his mind was made up.

September 20, 2016

Grandma had multiple doctor appointments each month, so I drove her when she didn't want to go by herself. Going over to her house on my own was strange at first; normally, I would have gone with both of my parents. Each time I saw Grandma, she would say, "I can't believe he would do this to you guys." "Don't worry," I would reply in reassurance, "We all have each other to get through this." What else could I say?

While sitting in the waiting room at the doctor's office, I thought of how strong Grandma was to keep up on her health so well. She was always independent and her family history was full of longevity. I hoped those qualities would make this time easier for her. Thankfully, during her meeting with the doctor, all her vitals checked out well. The medications she was prescribed, after her mild heart attack in June, controlled her heart health.

Since thinking of Dad always made her tear up, I never knew if she wanted to talk about him. Instead, I told her about the positives going on in my life. She always seemed pleased to hear good news. I did my best to reassure her that Mom and I had been moving forward. The one thing I didn't want her to suffer from was guilt. I reassured her that her son was no longer suffering. "We've got to keep on keeping on," she would say as we hugged goodbye.

Each time I left her, I'd get close to tears. When I saw my grandma, I saw my father; I'm sure people felt the same way when they saw me. That explains why some avoided coming over to our house. Grandma and Dad had similar mannerisms, such as their facial expressions, and the same eyes. Going through hardships at 89 years old is never easy. All I wanted for her was to be able to get through this.

I couldn't imagine how hard it was for her to suffer the loss of her child. Seeing Grandma made me angrier at Dad. She cried at the mention of his name and worried about Mom and I not being able to make ends meet. I told her worrying won't solve anything. To put his own, elderly mother through agony was unbelievable. Dad was distraught when he received the news of his mother's heart attack, and that was just a week before his first attempt. Maybe he was upset because that could interfere with his plans or that he caused it.

The anger re-surfaced when I thought of how she always called him "her rock." She was always comforted by knowing he would be there as she grew older. He was also the executor of her will; each time I went over to her house, she wanted to re-iterate her wishes for inherited items and financial preparations. It was incomprehensible that Dad put his mother through this horrific loss.

September 26, 2016

A meeting was about to be held, in a rented room at an office building, for the 45 investors of the company. Dad's friend, Stan, would talk about the massive debts, the alleged misappropriation of the money, and why there hadn't been any progress in the last year. The truth was going to come out. It wouldn't be easy for them when they had become accustomed to hearing positive updates each month. He never eluded that things were going in a different direction.

There weren't many meetings in recent years because, contrary to what Dad claimed, there hadn't been much to show. Progress stalled and investors wanted to know where their money went. Dad had received a lot of funding, but there was no concrete proof of recent progress.

Dad hadn't put the blame on himself for the sudden halt in the business. The only thing he admitted was that he naïvely put his faith in someone who promised success for his inventions. We weren't certain what was true or not, if that person really did brainwash him. I couldn't believe everything Dad said after the day of his first attempt; was it an exaggeration or was another source to blame for all the problems? He was too trusting, gave everyone the benefit of the doubt, and did business on handshakes.

Assuming he would now be the most hated man,

Dad withheld information that the investors needed to know about. With no money to continue what he promised, he saw the words "failure" above his head when looking into the mirror. He had never seen that throughout his life, he was always a hardworking man with success and admiration. People should remember my father for who he used to be: the brilliant man with a creative mind.

Once, while Dad was taking a shower, an idea came to him. He needed to write it down right away before it left him. He grabbed Mom's eyeliner pencil from the bathroom drawer and began to scribble on the side of the white shower wall. He drew his idea and wrote down the details of how a device for a home glaucoma reader could be engineered. It was quite a surprise for Mom to walk into the bathroom and see the design created from her makeup. She could not scrub it off until he got a picture of it.

Memories like that make me laugh and remember Dad as he was, not the villain people have made him out to be. Some investors were now calling my good-natured father a "con man." Did they think that Dad's ultimate plan was to waste their money and kill himself? They didn't know how hard he had struggled to please them or how difficult he had taken his failure. Many made large investments, expecting a great return, because they believed in Dad's ideas. They trusted the promises he made, but now felt betrayed. Dad had always planned on fulfilling those promises, but during the past year, there was roadblock after roadblock. In order to keep the investors optimistic, he kept them holding on while thinking everything would work out in the end. No one can say he didn't try.

Those that were close to Dad knew he had a big heart and only had good intentions to help others. Only 30 of the 45 investors came. Some were out of town while some chose not to attend. Dad's death still affected many, and they did not want to hear cruel things being said about their friend. I didn't want to attend the meeting either, I opted to prepare for it instead.

We decorated the room the same way we had with every investor meeting in the past. It was beautifully arranged with the food and layout of the chairs and tables. Stan had a presentation set up on his computer. He was going to answer questions from what we pieced together. It was not going to be pleasant.

Investors were starting to enter. I didn't know many, but they knew who I was. It wasn't until they said their names that I recognized them. I briefly talked with each person. No one offered condolences here, in fact, it felt like I should apologize to them. I grabbed food and left as soon as possible.

As I drove away, I felt relief but regretful that I left Mom. I had heard nothing but negativity the past few months from business associates. Most of which wrongly thought my father was a horrible person. There was only so much I could handle; no one wants to hear hateful things being said about their parent. I got home and idly watched TV, waiting for Mom to come home.

Hours passed by, the meeting went much longer than expected. I fought the urge to go to bed as it grew late. When I finally heard the garage door open, I went out to greet Mom. "How was it? What happened?" I asked while helping unload the car's trunk. It was filled with uneaten food and unopened drinks. No one appeared to have had an appetite. Mom was exhausted. I could tell the meeting took a toll on her. What she told me occurred was worse than what I had feared.

Investors yelled and swore after getting answers they did not want to hear. Not only did Mom have to sit through a meeting where horrible things were said about her recently deceased husband, but some turned around, pointing fingers at her, saying, "You should have known what was going on! You were his wife!" Worse yet, there were a few with a stake in the business that made scary threats. Little did they know, she was kept in the dark as much as they were. Mom was truly an innocent spouse who had as many questions as they did.

I had been excited for years to see Dad's products on the market, the ones that had made it were always a cause for celebration. It was unlikely we would see any of his recent inventions on store shelves. There were problems with ownership issues right before Dad passed; he let different parties believe they had ownership rights, making the mess worse.

Dad couldn't say "No." He wanted everyone to be satisfied and happy. What he had done was irresponsible; his generosity got him in a lot of trouble in business. Understandably, no one in the meeting saw the man that tried to give investors a great return on their money, just one that seemed careless. I could not imagine Dad standing in front of all of those people, admitting fault, saying everything that Stan was saying; he could no longer sugarcoat or hide things. He would have had to face all the accusations, the debt, and the loss of control of his dream business. He panicked when more pressure built, which caused him to make the mistakes that he did.

Hearing how the meeting went made me fluctuate between anger and understanding. Regardless of what actions Dad took, everyone would think less of him. I know why he did what he did, but I could not agree with him. There were multiple solutions, none of them pretty, but suicide should never have been an option.

September 30, 2016

It may seem silly, but I had grown increasingly superstitious of Fridays. Dad attempted suicide on a Friday, died on a Friday, and his funeral was on a Friday. Despite this creeping suspicion, Peter and I decided to try and break the streak.

We were headed to the beach with my dog. We had to cross over a long bridge, which would take us high above the bay towards the ocean. Right as we merged towards the bridge onramp, traffic slowed to a fraction of the speed limit. From that point, there was no way to exit. Ahead, we saw police cars and a small sedan pulled over. Police officers were looking over the edge of the bridge towards the water. As we neared, it was apparent that traffic wasn't stopped because of a car accident.

Cars slowly inched their way forward, the three-lane road was being funneled into a single lane. More so, everyone was driving slowly as they turned their heads, out of morbid curiosity, to see what was going on. As we got to the very front, just as we were about to drive past the scene, a police officer put his hand up to tell us to stop. He was standing directly in the center of the road, no way to pass him. They let a tow truck in to take the car away. Not too far to our right, a sign read "Suicide Counseling Crisis Team 24 hours" with the number 1-800-273-8255 below. The bridge has those signs posted throughout since it's notorious for suicides.

I looked over to watch what was going on, saying to Peter, "Oh my God. I cannot believe this is happening right now." Peter was frustrated, he had planned this excursion to get my mind off things for a few hours. Reality, it appeared, wasn't too eager to let me slip away. The two of us felt awkward. A civilian was talking to the officers. He was probably a witness. The doors and the trunk of the car were open, an officer searched through it. This was the only time I had ever seen the aftermath of a suicide. I imagined that this was the same protocol and scene on July 8th, high up in the mountains.

The police officer motioned for us to move forward, but I wanted to continue to watch what was going on. If allowed, I would have gone out there and talked to the officers. I wanted to tell them that this recently happened to me and ask them what they thought of the whole event. As we drove, Peter and I couldn't avoid talking about what we had seen. I told him, "Don't worry about it, it's hard for things to affect me anymore." He wasn't convinced, but it was true. Maybe if I hadn't dealt with a suicide this past year, it would have scarred me. Now, it was a little more than a curiosity to see the aftermath. Nothing surprised me anymore.

A thought that scared me was that one day, I would have to drive close to the bridge that Dad jumped off of. The drive to that remote mountain pass would be nerve-racking. Some of Dad's friends, however, visited the bridge to get closure; one of his friends even went to go see it the day after his passing. I searched for pictures of it on the Internet and found its location. The bridge is an architectural feat but also a magnet for suicides. Being below the flight path when flying into our city, doesn't make it easily avoidable. People have told Mom that they got an unsettling feeling while seeing it from the sky.

On large bridges, I started paying attention to the suicide crisis phone numbers. I wondered how many lives those have saved and if there was one on the bridge Dad jumped off of. A single life would be worth the cost of the sign. After Dad's death, I questioned myself: If I saw someone on the edge of the bridge, would I go out and talk to them? Would I be able to talk someone out of it? I, however, could not even stop my own father, how could I stop a stranger?

Anna Cambria

October 5, 2016

Mom and I kept up with our yoga practice. Focusing on breathing and doing the flowing poses soothed my body. Every time I rolled out my purple yoga mat on the gym floor, under the dimmed lights, my mind was put at ease. Not only was it a great exercise to de-stress, but my story wasn't known to anyone there. I felt incognito. No one cautiously approached me with a frown on their face asking, "So how are you holding up?" The only noises I heard were the instructor telling us what to do and the tranquil music over the speakers. Sanctuary.

Taking the dogs for a walk was another simple therapy, Peter and I did that the first night after Dad died. We developed a habit of going out only after dark. At that time the neighborhood is quiet, the roads lit only by streetlights. Our walks reminded me of seeing my parents walking our neighborhood together in the past. Sometimes, when driving home from work or school, I would see them together holding hands. They were the cutest couple, continuing to have genuine love for each other after 33 years of marriage. Others would say that they were the ideal couple; I had always hoped to have a marriage like theirs.

Although I was keeping up with physical health, signs of stress were showing on my body. It became evident that keeping emotions locked inside was harmful. My brush would pull small clumps of hair at a time. The amount of strands on my hands after washing my hair dramatically increased. It devastated me because my thick, wavy hair was part of my identity. Acne spotted up all over my cheeks as well, like a fire that couldn't be extinguished. To release these toxic emotions causing physical degradation, I decided on therapy. I had nothing to lose.

My hospital offered individual and group therapy, but I chose individual to focus on myself. When I called to schedule a few days prior, there was fortunately a last minute cancellation for this day. To prepare for the therapy session, I wrote down notes on my phone in case my mind blanked on what to discuss.

I was anxious for my first appointment. As I walked around the buildings, I found signs for psychiatry, the area that the nurses told me to check in at. I never thought I would go to that department for myself. I chose a hospital location different than the one Dad went to so there would not be reminders of the past.

People of all ages occupied the waiting room. There were teenagers with their parents, a few girls around my age, and men dressed as if they had come straight from work. The men there reminded me of Dad. It wasn't too surprising; the largest demographic of suicide victims are middle-aged, white men. I wondered what each person was there for. It made me glad that people were willing to seek help for themselves.

When checking in to my appointment, the woman at the front desk handed me an electronic tablet. On it was a wellness exam. They told me that before each appointment, patients take the same survey to monitor their state of mind. As I took the exam, I patiently waited for the therapist to enter the waiting room to call my name.

Ten minutes later, a man walked out to introduce himself. He seemed kind as we talked while walking out of the waiting area. This first session was primarily for him to get to know me. Once we got into the room, I recounted the events of Dad's suicide. I hadn't shared that story for a while, and it made me cry the hardest I had in a long time. Being a therapist, he must have heard some hardships in his line of work, but he seemed astonished by mine. I went into therapy thinking I wanted guidance on how to control anger, but I ended up uncovering and releasing the self-hidden agony. Emotions arose in me that I didn't even know were buried.

A technique was introduced to me called "The empty chair," where one talks to the chair as if their loved one is sitting in it. I would have to communicate my feelings and say what I wished to say to Dad; it would not consist of mild words. I told my therapist I couldn't do it. Looking at the chair, imagining Dad sitting there in spirit, made me choke up. Instead of pushing, he suggested expressing my feelings out loud when home alone. My dogs would probably think I am crazy for talking when there is no one around. Throughout my school years I practiced speeches with them as my test audience, though they often got bored of my rambling and left my room in the middle of it.

As I walked out to my car, I felt lighter. My eyes were red and sore from crying, but the ball of stress confined inside my chest melted away. Anger towards Dad had turned to grief. I had taken steps back and was right where I started in July; I wanted the sadness to be released, not to experience it all over again. Perhaps confronting what I buried was beneficial to my mental health. Instead of dealing with it earlier, I rushed to heal.

Dad didn't accept therapy the same way I did. He was able to see in his group how traumatic suicidal actions are, but he was in too much pain himself to go on living. I read about individuals who went to suicide bereavement groups, often with a family member, because seeing the pain of others might motivate them to overcome their suicidal thoughts. Their ability to admit something was wrong showed bravery. Some people don't discuss or attend therapy because it has a stigma to it; pride can get in the way of healing.

Maybe if Dad saw the pain of loved ones he thought would hate him, it would have been different. I began to wonder how much other people were affected by his decision. He didn't just shake up the lives of Mom and me, he shook up the lives of everyone who knew him. All the people I saw crying over Dad's death didn't "get over it" within a few days. All the daughters and sons who grew worried that they could lose a parent the same way I did couldn't change their fears. Everyone was shaken up.

Witnessing Dad's friends in tears and blaming themselves for not being able to help was difficult. They claimed, "I thought we were friends" and "He should have come to me first," wishing there could have been an opportunity to talk. They didn't think of him as a defeated man, only someone who was a good friend. They would have been there had he been able to be honest and not let pride get in the way.

October 21, 2016

On this Friday evening, Mom and I were driving back home on the freeway after a movie and dinner with friends when, suddenly, traffic slowed almost to a stop. Traffic accidents are pretty common on this busy freeway, so we didn't think too much of it. As we inched on, I noticed a car was parked at the center of a tall overpass running over the road we were on. A police car was behind it. I had a sick feeling in my stomach. I checked my phone to look at the traffic on the maps app. A red line of traffic appeared all the way until the bridge.

The closest off-ramp was after the scene, so we couldn't exit. After my recent experience witnessing the aftermath of the suicide with Peter, it wasn't too hard to guess what took place a mile ahead of us. I grew anxious that Mom was with me; I didn't want to say anything to scare her. The parked car stayed stationary after the police car backed away. What would we have seen if we had left the mall ten minutes earlier?

We inched closer and closer, at a slow ten miles per hour. Once again, I found myself driving past the scene of a suicide bridge jumper. Looking to the side of the road, I was left staggered. On the ground, right under the bridge and surrounded by police, was a white cloth. It covered a lump roughly the size of a human body.

"It looks like a suicide," I said, "Something on the ground was covered." After a moment of silence, Mom simply responded, "That's pretty devastating..." The rest of the ride home was quiet. It was unbelievable that after never witnessing something like that before, I encountered it twice shortly after my father's similar death. I texted Rita and Peter about it, who both expressed sympathy for Mom and me, but I was thinking about the family and friends of the person who died. I felt their loss and wished them strength.

That was someone's child, someone's best friend, someone's family member, or possibly someone's spouse or parent laying on the ground. It might have been unexpected or maybe that person struggled with depression. Now those left behind would go through the grief, the therapy, and the struggle of living life again. Each death impacts numerous people.

It would have been mortifying to be the drivers on the freeway who witnessed the person fall to their death. An incredible amount of respect should go to police officers. Their profession is one of the most difficult emotionally and physically. Police are the first responders to scenes like this and learn to cope with the constant trauma. I will never know how Dad's death affected the officer who saw it. He ended up never coming over; we partly believe that it could have been too hard for him to face the survivors of the man he witnessed jumping off a bridge.

November 24, 2016

The first major holiday without Dad was Thanksgiving. Michael and Leah invited us over to their house to celebrate with their family as well as Mom's brother, Uncle John, and his wife, Aunt Louise. Immediately after walking through the door, we could smell the wonderful food. Casseroles and mashed potatoes, turkey with stuffing, several different types of pies, and all the wonderful staples of Thanksgiving lined the counter. Being surrounded by family lessened the pain and made the day pleasant.

We sat around the large table and enjoyed dinner. We talked about vacations, funny memories, and exciting future plans. Mom even brought over a large bin of old family pictures. Even with the distraction of family, food, and holiday merriment, Dad's absence remained painfully obvious. Everyone was respectful and avoided talking about him when they could, but his charisma was missed. It was as if the larger family dynamic was thrown off. His jokes, his place at the table, and his unique style of conversing were no longer present.

December 11, 2016

It had been a few days since Dad's birthday. Every year, Mom planned something fun for it; she even threw him several surprise parties in the past. Looking at our calendar in our home office, Dad's birth date remained blank. There was no special celebration with friends and family this year, nor will there ever be one again. His birthday date will only be a hardship now. To help get through the day, we went to the movie theater to see a comedy. Seeing a movie was a good escape because it distracted our minds for a few hours.

Dad's recent birthday caused me to think of him more. December 2015 was the beginning of his downward spiral, according to him. I wasn't around as much towards the end of his life because of school and work. During those two weeks, between his first attempt and suicide, I regretted my decision to remove myself from him. He had described me as "launched," thinking I didn't need him now that I'm an adult. I should have shown how much I valued our relationship and cared about him. I'd never be able to tell him that he needed to stay.

These thoughts raced through my mind and caused me to feel especially low during this average day in December. I was home alone and started talking out loud, as my therapist instructed, in hopes of alleviating some of the guilt. I needed a sign that Dad was listening.

As I rambled, a wind-up toy on a shelf in my room went off. It hadn't been touched in years but it started playing on its own. The jingle of it startled me. In my surprise, I harshly yelled: "Stop." The noise and motion of the toy stopped on command. After a moment of contemplation, I refused to believe it was anything but a sign from Dad. That experience told me everything I needed to know. He was listening.

December 24, 2016

We didn't send out annual Christmas cards. We always placed a family picture inside the card, and it included our dogs. It had always been near impossible to get both dogs looking at a camera, so we had to be creative. In order to get them looking up, we threw a pen in the direction of the camera right before the timer went off. We got laughs from the many outtakes throughout the years.

Continuing other traditions, without guilt, allowed me to enjoy my favorite holiday season. I loved driving around neighborhoods to see the lights. Seeing Santa at the mall, decorated trees, ornaments, and ice skating rinks around the city, put me in the Christmas spirit. I ignored the dark feeling that told me I should be mourning instead.

Each year we had put up lights on the inside and outside of our house, so Mom once again decorated beautifully to make it festive. After donating our old one, we bought a new tree and placed new ornaments on it. While opening the tree decoration bin earlier in December, I came across the "World's Best Dad" and my parents' "First Christmas Together" ornaments. I turned a blind eye to those and left them wrapped in the bin. The ornaments that made the tree festive were not going to be ones that remind me of the obvious void. Seeing personalized ornaments brought back memories. While decorating the tree last year,

I never would have imagined that that'd be the last Christmas with the three of us. It made me question how different life will be when I decorate the tree in 2017.

Mom and I celebrated Christmas Eve at my cousin Kathy's house. She had a lot of family over, including Uncle John and Aunt Louise. We made a great time out of the night. Everyone sat around a large table and had a delicious meal. There was no mention of anything sad that night; it was a night of celebration. After dinner, everyone partook in a white elephant gift exchange, swapping gifts and not knowing what they will go home with. I ended up with seashell-shaped candles and Mom won a coffee mug with a "California" design. We were happy.

We all had a special Christmas Eve. It was odd to be celebrating another holiday without Dad. I felt less of an absence than I did on Thanksgiving, but the following morning could be hard. Maybe this celebration wasn't too lonely because I have grown accustomed to going to events, traveling, or living life with just Mom. Am I beginning to adapt to my new normal?

December 25, 2016

I dragged my feet down the hall to the living room, still in my pajamas, to open gifts. Christmas felt a little different this year with one less stocking on the fireplace. No "From: Dad" or "To: Dad" presents were under the tree. Gifts from Mom felt more emotional to receive. After gifts and lunch, we kept the tradition of going to Mass. The Christmas service was my favorite to attend. Hearing Christmas carols and seeing the decorations around the church brought me joy.

A neighbor who lived a block away knocked on our door in the early afternoon. In her arms was a blanket as a gift for Dad. He had helped her locate her lost cat multiple times and wanted to thank him. She had also brought over peanut butter balls that she made. Unknown to her, that was one of Dad's favorite desserts. She was not aware of the news of his passing and was devastated when we told her. It was miserable to ruin someone's Christmas day.

The remainder of the day, Mom and I stayed home. It was the most notably different holiday, but we made the best of it. I thought of how different Christmas would be the following years. They could only get easier from here, or maybe the further away we get, the more difficult.

Anna Cambria

.

December 31, 2016

Peter and I spent New Year's Eve together at a little restaurant and returned home to watch the countdown. Watching the numbers drop was more exciting than ever. Mercifully, 2016 was drawing to an end. Surprisingly, it had gone by quickly. Back in July, in the midst of the fallout of losing Dad, I imagined the end of the year would slowly inch on, but instead the days had raced by.

That's not to say it had been easier than expected, rather, we made the challenge manageable. We still had plenty of difficulties, known and unknown, ahead. For example, Mom and I still ran into people who had not heard of Dad's death. It had been tricky; sometimes we would be caught unaware that an acquaintance did not know, but other times, we would be surprised by the amount of information strangers had found out. I was fine with a few acquaintances not knowing; there was no need to devastate them.

We became better storytellers while the listeners always had that same, sympathetic look. They usually said, "We need to get together soon" or if I wasn't around, "I'll reach out to your daughter." Neither of those would ever happen, though; either they were too afraid or didn't know how to proceed. I didn't hold it against them.

My goal for 2017 was to make it a new beginning

and have a better attitude towards life. A new year was not just a new chapter to me, it was a new book. I could not put 2016 completely behind me, however, because things from this year would bleed into next. My fears and anxiety would remain while Mom was still forced to be associated with the business. It had been almost six months and there hadn't been progress with moving the company forward. On top of that, threats and credit card companies continued to haunt us.

The future scared me. I couldn't think about long-term goals. From experience, the best advice I had followed was turning my attention to the present and letting the future come on its own time. If I thought about it being unpredictable, the present would be soured, which in turn spoils the future. I had to remember to take care of myself in the now. The rest of my life doesn't have to be full of misery and unhappiness.

February 20, 2017

Every step, no matter how small, was significant when it came to healing. For example, for the first time in over seven months, I was able to listen to music before going to sleep. In the past, if I wasn't tired when trying to fall asleep, or if I had a stressful day, music helped calm me. This night, I put my headphones in and didn't have to turn off a song seconds into it. Recently, any song made the already depressing, lonely nights worse; I was enjoying myself instead of mourning Dad. Maybe my mind associated music with the painful times this past summer. I would often play music while preparing for my day. It's what I was doing on June 24th when I got the call from Mom telling me that Dad was taken away by an ambulance.

Although this milestone was a step in the right direction, I was only able to listen to music in small increments, not a full playlist at a time. It could be due to life fluctuating between happiness and sadness. I could be having a wonderful day, then get hit when remembering other things that are going on in my life. How could one go through life unfazed when trials for your deceased father's company were still occurring, karma wasn't being served for those your father claimed harassed him, and your mother and her attorneys negotiate every day with the IRS and creditors for debts Mom wasn't aware of?

April 8, 2017

Mom belonged to a bereavement group called Survivors of Suicide Loss. She had been going to meetings once a month ever since December. In April, they held their annual survivors of suicide workshop. The event was intended to help others meet those in their similar position, as well as find ways to recover in a healthy manner. Mom had signed both of us up for it. I was reluctant to go, telling her, "I'm over being sad. All this will do is make me cry." I planned to back out, but decided to get out of my comfort zone and join; I have tried to say "yes" to more things now.

After arriving, we signed in and got name tags. Breakfast food lined the tables in the back but I didn't have much of an appetite due to nerves and uncertainty of what we would be doing. A table was set up with bead necklaces of various colors; each color represented who you lost. I picked up the gold necklace, it corresponded to the loss of a parent. I looked around to see if many others had gold necklaces but there was only one other so far. The most common were white, the loss of a child.

Seating wasn't assigned, so Mom and I sat down at a table near the center. The woman next to Mom lost her son and the woman next to me had lost her daughter. It was the first time I've conversed with others in my situation. Being surrounded by other survivors of suicide gave everyone a sense of solidarity. The common ground between us gave a sense of connection; shared struggles often form quick and strong bonds. To a certain extent, we all knew how each other felt.

We were asked to place a picture of our deceased loved one on the table so everyone could see what they looked like. For our first activity, we had to turn to a stranger sitting next to us and tell them a favorite memory. I started tearing up when recalling "Dad and Daughter Days," unable to finish my story. The woman I was conversing with told me about what she and her daughter did for fun.

It added emotion seeing pictures of the individuals behind the survivor's tragic story. Each image represented a separate, distinct life that ended prematurely. We were sitting next to the people who displayed and carried heartbreak because of their loved one's decision to end their life.

Looking at the picture I had of Dad, I saw someone I held dear to my heart, but his image also made me angry. No one had a way of guessing that the happy man, smiling at the camera, would commit suicide someday. If one compared pictures of Dad from five years ago to the more recent ones, it would appear work was taking a toll. His smile was not as bright and beaming as it used to be. He looked physically stressed, but in reality, he had great physical health, claiming he was "as active and athletic as a 20-year-old" with a long life ahead; now his bicycles and weights were in our garage collecting dust.

Throughout the workshop, speakers shared their stories and everyone participated in activities for reminiscing about their loved one. At the end, we broke off into small groups of who lost a parent, significant other, sibling, child, or friend. I was wary of the group discussion at first, but in the end, it turned out to be a great experience.

A moderator began the hour-long discussion and from then on, he let us take it over. There were many minute-long pauses when no one knew what to say, but everyone did well throughout. It was amazing that we had been through the exact same thing. I was proud of myself for being confident enough to participate, unusual for me in group settings. Opening up to them was easier for me as opposed to opening up to friends and family. All survivors are different, but we are able to understand what each other has gone through. I saw the pain in their eyes, the frown on their faces, and heard their voices grow shaky. It made me cry. Although the workshop was emotionally draining, I was glad that Mom signed us both up.

It was still unbelievable to me, even if almost a year's time had passed, that I would have to attend an event like this. While at home during the day, it seemed like Dad was still at work. I couldn't stop my false belief that he would walk down the hallway or come in through the front door at night. Since he was taken abruptly from my life, it had been hard to get out of that habit. I finally began to grow accustomed to everything just being about Mom and me, no longer "my parents and me." If anything, it began to feel odd to say "my parents."

April 16, 2017

     A lot of the hype had died down by now. People had begun treating Mom and me normally again. I didn't receive looks of pity or hear, "I'm sorry," every time I saw someone who knew our story. Friends and family now tell us, "You are both so strong," after watching our transitions over the year. Some still felt the need to talk about Dad, it helped them come to terms with his death.

     Although it was great that the spotlight had moved away, people expected us to have moved on by now. Mom and I still were healing but many assumed we should now be living the "normal" way of life that they are. Even though we appeared better, every day there had been emotional hardships. Adding to the pain of loss, all of the "firsts" without Dad were not over yet.

     Easter fell on the same day as my parents' 34th wedding anniversary this year. Although Mom and I lost the same person, we couldn't know exactly how each other was feeling since we both had a different relationship with Dad. I wouldn't know how much one suffers a loss on their usually celebrated wedding anniversary. Regardless, Mom is the strongest person. With her guiding us, we have held up well. She still lit their unity candle as she did each anniversary with hopes and prayers for the following year. The candle has their wedding invitation on both sides of the white wax pillar.

It was a blessing in disguise that we were able to put our attention on a holiday instead of a painful reminder. Leah invited us over for Easter dinner. We celebrated our faith and didn't mention the anniversary, not because we were trying to overlook the pain, but because Mom wanted to celebrate the holiday. Easter is a big day of celebration for Catholics, and that's what we turned our attention to.

Mom and I had been lucky to have our faith during tough anniversaries. Anyone can easily back away from God and the church when something of this magnitude happens, or it validates their belief that there is no God. The best way I found peace and acceptance was through religion or spirituality. Turning to my faith in God helped reduce my anger. I was determined to not let that anger and anxiety change my identity or cause me to lose my trust in God.

Mom and I tried to focus on the good and blessings of each day; that was all we could do. Life had not been easy but I've been growing into a stronger individual. I will see Dad again in heaven; as a Catholic, there's never been a doubt in my mind about that. Sometimes that thought, however, angers me. Dad is in heaven, without a worldly worry, while Mom and I are stuck with the fallout he caused. To be fair, he was living in hell for a long time and had troubles throughout his life that he kept to himself. He only ever watched "happy" movies (his favorite was Groundhog Day), and couldn't handle movies with sad plots; maybe they were relatable when reflecting on his own childhood.

May 4, 2017

I decided that this fourth therapy session was going to be my last. It was one of the most beneficial things for my healing process, but I didn't feel the need to continue talking about it as deep as I had each time. During the last session, tears flowed from my eyes only once; there wasn't anything new to talk about.

My wonderful therapist had assisted me with healing in a different way, but I had a main source of therapy: writing. Relaying my feelings onto paper over the year had helped me reflect on myself. It forced me to stop and think about the causes, effects, and people that had been involved. The feelings I wrote down during January were much different than the feelings I had now. I have been able to accept what happened, hate the action that Dad did, and still love the person he was. It is hard to predict, however, how I'm going to feel in the future when Dad isn't with me for important milestones; luckily a major one occurred two months before he passed.

Exactly a year ago, I was studying for my final exams and eager to graduate. Mom and I had been under the impression that that was why Dad hid secrets from us. He wanted me to be able to graduate college without seeing my parents distressed about money. It was my last semester and I would have felt the need to get a full time job, maybe even two, and drop out of school.

I felt refreshed after getting home from that final session. When I went into my room to lay down, I looked at the framed picture on my shelf that was taken right after my graduation ceremony. I am wearing my cap and gown with my parents to each side of me. In that framed picture is a smiling, 22-year-old woman, who doesn't know that her life is about to be devastated by the man standing next to her. It was one of the best days but I could no longer reflect on it without feeling sad. I couldn't get myself to take down pictures of him, even though looking at them hurt. It would have made me feel like I was erasing his memory or didn't care about him anymore. Although many bear the consequences of his actions, I'd still give anything to see him even if it was for a few moments.

June 18, 2017

This was my first Father's Day without a father. In previous years, the three of us would go out to lunch at one of Dad's favorite restaurants followed by a movie or other activity of Dad's choice. Now, it was another day of forced reflection. Father's day, the anniversary of Dad's first suicide attempt, and his death date are all within a few weeks of each other.

When I woke up, there was no dread, the day didn't feel any different. This day was going to be a normal day, not a holiday. I was far from the only person in the world who was fatherless. Mom and I went out to have a champagne brunch at our favorite Mexican restaurant. Surprisingly, no Father's Day decorations were in sight. There were big families sitting at tables nearby, but it didn't bother me. I was enjoying my huevos rancheros too much to focus on anything else. We didn't find it necessary to bring up Dad. The past few months he became less of a discussion topic to everyone.

All my friends and family had been respectful, but I still worried that I would receive texts saying, "How are you doing?" or "Hope you're OK today." It would make me feel like I should feel guilty going about my day. Seeing posts about Father's Day on social media didn't affect me, nor did talking to others about what they were doing for this day. If

Father's Day had occurred a month or two after Dad's passing, it would have been incredibly hard. I had time to adapt.

What most are not aware of is that I don't associate my father with suicide. That wasn't what defined him nor should it be to anyone else. One of my biggest annoyances has been when people tiptoe around subjects they worry I might find difficult. For example, friends often stiff up in awkwardness if someone mentions the word suicide or if a suicide occurs in a movie or TV show that we are watching. In reality, it does not release dark memories, it's just awkward. Dad is gone, and I miss him severely, but suicide doesn't trigger any pain in me. A ringtone he had, things that interested him, places we visited together, or activities we used to do are what remind me of him.

The rest of my life I will be surrounded by the mention of suicide or hearing the term used loosely. There is no avoiding that. While I do wish that suicide wasn't the subject of jokes, I understand it is something that I will have to deal with. In the end, it's simply a decision between growing stronger and remembering Dad how he was, or being afraid of a word. I choose to remember Dad fondly.

June 24, 2017

Mom and I still dealt with the blowback of Dad's suicide when we stumbled upon the one-year anniversary of his first attempt. The only reason I was glad this day had arrived was because it would be over in 24 hours. The "firsts" without Dad had been successfully navigated, such as the first holidays and birthdays. It hadn't been an easy journey, but Dad would have been proud of how well I handled my life. I had grown healthier and became more open to new opportunities.

While many things had changed within a year's time, some things remained the same. People were still in shock and were confused as to why such a happy man could do this. Multiple former business associates of Dad displaced their anger towards Mom. Occasionally, the subject would cool until a new issue popped up and caused the anger to flare. In this case, one of Dad's businesses had been forced to shut down a few days prior. It was a blessing for us. I had been "over it" and wanted to be done seeing Mom relive this nightmare. Engineers came to the conclusion that creating a prototype of one of Dad's products was not possible without the knowledge of his technology secrets. The project was deemed unviable, at least for the intention he devised it for.

Nearly a decade spent on creating the device turned

out to be in vain. The trials for the company were over, the prototypes had to be scrapped, but finding out where all the missing money went became an unsolved mystery. In the suicide note, Dad claimed it was misappropriation by the person he named as his harasser. People would eventually give up trying to figure it out.

Investors were irate. They unjustifiably lashed out at Mom through emails. Threats had begun once again. Although we were not sure if they could do so, it caused stress to escalate more during this already hard day. The business could not be left in the past while the problems were never-ending.

I had to continue my mantra of focusing on one day at a time. Being the anniversary of the tragedy, I focused on getting through it. Doing what we could to cope with the knowledge of further hardships, Mom and I ran around to do some errands to stay busy. While driving, we could no longer avoid the obvious. We talked about the past year and the future. "Look how far we've come from a year ago," I told her. We were each healing on our own time, some days better than others, but we were the only ones who understood each other; our friends and family had never been through the same trauma. We had scarcely gone a day without talking about Dad. Our discussions were usually filled with upset.

I thought of the night exactly a year ago, it was a drastic difference. Last year, hot stress raced up and down my body, waking me up throughout the night. The image of Dad in his hospital bed, saying, "I can't provide for my family anymore," ran through my mind. It was the worst night of my life. We swore to keep secrets about the severity of the business debts and Dad's suicide attempt. I have always wondered if telling close family or friends after his first attempt would've helped him recover. On the other hand, maybe Mom and I would have blamed ourselves, thinking we drove him to commit suicide by embarrassing him. He was always concerned about how he came across to others. He could not see himself being happy when we didn't have the money that he constantly promised from his inventions. There would have been a way to get back on our feet, even if it took a few years consisting of uphill battles.

He could not live with himself and face his wife and daughter every day, knowing how much havoc and devastation he caused. If Dad was still alive after a second attempt, it would be more stressful than the two weeks after his first. Would we not let him drive for the rest of his life? Could we ever leave him home alone? We would never trust him. Nonetheless, if Dad was still here, I would have an amazing father in my life.

Anna Cambria

.

July 8, 2017 – Reflecting on the Year

Mom went to visit Dad's memorial at the mausoleum. I hadn't returned since the service a year ago. I believe I will eventually return, but not in the near future. That's not where I think of him being. When I am there, it reminds me of the pain from last summer, not the joy Dad brought me in life. Later in the day, Mom, Peter, and I went to dinner with my cousins Michael, Leah, Mark, and Cody. We had a nice time while enjoying our Italian pasta dishes.

Exactly a year ago, we had spent the afternoon and night with Michael and Leah at our house. The setting and feeling that night was the complete opposite of what it was at this dinner; we were able to smile now. There was no need to talk about our financial future, scared of how we were going to deal with it, because our life seemed to be moving forward steadily. Some things were still unresolved in Dad's company, but we fought to distance ourselves from it.

The year had gone by fast. I had made great progress in my healing but backslid at times. The shock was still there and how Dad died still made it hard to accept. I missed his laugh and hugs. He always called me "Pumpkin," and I hadn't been able to hear him call me that for some time. My own father had become a distant memory to me as if he has been gone for five years. The only time I talked to him was in my dreams. There is no mention of death in those dreams, but the three of us lack cohesiveness. Throughout the dream, the sky is dark and cloudy. I did not want to continue dreaming about him as often as I had been. It only took me to the past the more he was in my mind.

I wish I didn't have to go through something as hard as this, especially at such a young age, but I didn't have a choice. The only option was to continue with life and immediately adapt. Survivors of suicide loss experience psychological trauma, often reliving their nightmare each day. I had feared becoming an unlikeable person because of my anxiety. I worried about losing another loved one. I have had times where something reminded me of Dad, such as a phrase he used to say, and it triggered sadness. It had been challenging to stop myself from texting a picture to Dad if I saw something he would like.

I get asked how I've been able to cope so well, and my answer has always been, "By surrounding myself with a great support system." Michael and Leah were there for us whenever we needed them. Uncle Anthony stayed with us to assist with various tasks around the house. Rita would drop anything to come help. Callie, Jessica, and Mac were a great second family to me. Peter was by my side every day when I was at my lowest; we had only been together for a little over a year before Dad died, so our relationship was forced to mature quickly. Most importantly, I am incredibly thankful for Mom, the strongest person I know. I walk through life with a genuine smile because of all of them. There was strengthening in my relationships, others' relationships were mended, and my faith in humanity was strong.

From the support of those around me, and my newfound confidence, I can overcome any obstacle life throws at me. Pushing through the turmoil made me stronger. I wanted goals, vacations, and events to look forward to. I wrote out a list of what I wanted to do in life, my top one being to travel to all fifty states in the US. I made sure to plan fun things for the future that allowed me to see the positives. I need to be thankful for what I have rather than dwelling on what I don't.

Everyone who goes through tragedy has their own way of grieving. My way is not better or worse than another woman in her 20s who has been through a similar experience. If needed, there are great resources to turn to for depression and suicidal thoughts. They are available 24 hours a day. Know that you are not alone in this struggle. Anyone would do anything in their power to aid you in overcoming hardships, even if you think they wouldn't. Please, seek help when you need it. The world is a better place with you in it.

Suicide Prevention Lifeline: 1-800-273-8255

CONCLUSION

Over the year, I met many people who had previously known someone that committed suicide. I hated hearing how common it was because everyone is affected by it, not just immediate family. Dad's friends, Mom's friends, and my friends were impacted more than I would have imagined. I still get haunted by the cries I heard on the phone and the image of adults tearing up in front of me. People experienced complete shock.

In order to heal, I learned that one needs to move on from anger towards their loved one, God, or anyone they may put blame on. I still have trouble with anger when thinking about what Dad put our family and friends through, but anger has slowly begun evolving into compassion. Others may react in another way: sadness, apathy, or something else entirely. Every situation is unique, but dealing with the emotions in a healthy way is the first, best, and most helpful step.

I came across a quote, by Shakti Gawain, that applied well to my story and emotions, "The practice of engaging in affirmations allows us to begin replacing some of our stale, worn out, negative mind chatter with more positive ideas and concepts." I can't continue seeing my own father, and my future, in a negative light. For the most part, I have won my internal battle and can now see the future as something bright, once again.

Even if I still get angry at Dad, I wouldn't have wanted anyone else as a father. I miss him constantly and he is in my heart every day. It seems like a never-ending battle with emotions. Life will get better though. Progress is slow, unnoticeable on a day to day scale, but looking over the period of months, it is significant. Everything will eventually fall into place, even if it takes a few years to get there.

It is important to not feel guilty about going on with your fun, future plans or how you choose to grieve. I learned to accept grief when I feel it and enjoy living life. I am still going to pursue my dreams and will not let this tragedy dictate who I am for the worse. Holding in negativity was unhealthy because it made me an angry person. I shouldn't have hate towards my father forever.

It was not Dad who took his life, it was a hidden illness that no one could have seen or prevented. We are aware of visible diseases such as cancer lumps, deformities, abnormal test results, or any visual signs that accompany suffering. Those are easier to accept because we see them with our eyes and know it wasn't their fault. Depression and suicidal thoughts are very similar, but we don't see the physical signs of suffering, they are completely internal and do not show up on scans or in blood tests. In addition, the pain we perceive doesn't match the intensity or depth of the actual sickness. I have heard or read that people ask why someone suffering from depression doesn't snap out of it or focus on happy thoughts. That statement shows the widespread ignorance of mental health issues. One cannot choose to feel happy during low times any more than one can wish away a broken bone.

No one knows what is going on in a stranger's life. I give people the benefit of the doubt when I can. If I see someone acting rude or have an attitude, I try not to condemn them for it. It can be difficult, but everyone has a battle they are fighting.

The story of losing my father to suicide is one that I have grown used to telling, but it still seems unreal. It isn't a pleasant story, nor a common topic of discussion. That said, I believe it demonstrates the process of discovering, reacting, and eventually overcoming a tragedy.

Pray for yourself and take the time that you need to grieve. Death is an inevitable part of life, but humans have the power to rebuild. Nothing will ever be able to replace a loved one, nothing can bring them back, but their memory is a gift unto itself, and accepting that is learning to live with our new normal.

Anna Cambria

A poem written by Dad in 2010:

To A Wonderful Life

I can't imagine a more beautiful life
Two angels, a daughter and wife

The love and the laughter I hear from you two
It fills our home and my heart so true

You both bring so much joy for this world to see
It inspires all others how it is to be

So much love and devotion, hard work and play
It's a job well done at the end of the day

You are both everything to me, my loving treasure
As a husband and father it just doesn't get any better

Love Dad

Made in the USA
San Bernardino, CA
23 January 2020